MADE FOR LEARNING

Education

MADE FOR LEARNING

How the Conditions of Learning Guide Teaching Decisions

Debra Crouch and Brian Cambourne

Richard C. Owen Publishers, Inc.
Katonah, New York

Credits:
Page 114 illustrations from Spiders by J. Feely. Copyright © 2009 by Okapi Educational Publishing. Published by Okapi Educational Publishing, Temecula, CA. Reprinted by permission of the Publisher. All rights reserved.

Pages 135-137 from *Building Bigger Ideas: A Process for Teaching Purposeful Talk* by Maria Nichols. Copyright © 2019 by Maria Nichols. Published by Heinemann, Portsmouth, NH. Reprinted by permission of the Publisher. All rights reserved.

Library of Congress Cataloging-in-Publication,
Control Number: 2014941670

ISBN 978-1-878450-00-5 pb
ISBN 978-1-878450-01-2 ebook

Richard C. Owen Publishers, Inc.
P.O. Box 585
Katonah, New York 10536
914 232-3903 (phone)
914 232-3977 (fax)
www.RCOwen.com

The text type was set in Baskerville and Helvetica Neue
Design/production credit: Ginny Tormey, Digital Arts Professional

Printed in the United States of America
9 8 7 6 5 4 3 2 1

For more information about our professional books and our children's books (in English and Spanish), visit our website at www.RCOwen.com or call 1-800-336-5588.

Debra Crouch
In loving memory of Pam Reed
You embodied what it meant to be a well-read educator,
a well-informed human being, and a well-loved friend.

Brian Cambourne
To my faithful mate, Ned
He leaves his warm bed and snoozes under my desk
in the early hours of the morning when I write.
He is both a comfort and a de facto "conference partner."

Table of Contents

More to the Story—Listed by Title

Brian's Story

In 1988, I published my first book, *The Whole Story: Natural Learning and the Acquisition of Literacy in the Classroom.*

After three decades, I still remember putting a lot of thought into my title and subtitle. The reference to *The Whole Story* was intended to be a clever contextual pun that reflected the competing theories of literacy learning being hotly debated at the time. In the 1980s, I'd developed a professional reputation as an advocate of a holistic approach to teaching and learning literacy. The intended message embedded in my main title was: *This book will deliver the real or full (i.e., "whole") story about holistic theories of learning and teaching.*

There were two intended messages embedded in the subtitle. The first was metaphorical: *This book will tell the whole story by explaining how a theory called Natural Learning will "liberate" teachers who had become "prisoners" of an outdated and flawed theory of learning that created barriers to effective learning.*

The second was more practical in nature: *Teachers who are prepared to adopt the principles of Natural Learning and apply them to their classroom practices will remove these barriers, thus making learning to read and write less complicated.* Both messages, I felt, were powerful and invigorating!

Essentially, the overall purpose of the book was to persuade teachers that the knowledge they needed to "acquire" in order to apply the principles of holistic teaching to their classrooms could be found in three overlapping domains of research and theory, namely:

- the **conditions** of learning that supported young children learning to talk;

- effective reading and writing **processes**; and

- how to turn these **conditions** and **processes** into **effective pedagogy**.

Ultimately, the structure and content of the book reflected my attempt to develop a coherent and cohesive amalgam of the complex principles inherent in these three domains of concern. As a professional book, it was relatively successful. It stayed in print until 1995, and the royalties helped me pay off my mortgage a few years earlier than I expected.

So, after thirty-plus years since publication, why do I think a new book is necessary? The simple answer is that while I still believe the theory of learning and the underlying processes of reading and writing I presented in *The Whole Story* are valid, I've learned, in the intervening years, that many readers found it difficult to turn these theories of learning into classroom practice. While teachers would nod enthusiastically about the content of the book and assure me they "got" it, when I observed in their classrooms, I found significant mismatches between what they claimed to understand about learning and their classroom practices. Why? What made turning the Conditions of Learning into effective classroom practice so difficult?

As I've continued to spend time in classrooms and engage in conversations with other educators, I've come to believe that a basic tenet of my original thinking was inadequate. In 1988, although I was aware of how language choice could shape the intended meanings an author wanted a text to communicate, I was theoretically ignorant about how the deep, almost covert, metaphors embedded in discourse could affect thinking and behavior. And my inadequate thinking was perpetuated by my choice of language and discourse. Over the course of the past thirty years, what I've come to believe is that, as long as we (teachers and myself) continue to speak of knowledge as something "acquired," we will continue to teach in ways that reflect a transmission model of learning, regardless of our voiced philosophical viewpoints. If we truly believe in constructivist models of learning and holistic models of teaching, we must also believe that learners construct their own meanings; they don't "acquire" them. And, if we believe that learners don't "acquire" meanings, then our Discourse of Acquisition must also change. If we continue to talk of knowledge and meanings as though they are "stuff" we can acquire, our embedded thinking about learning and teaching will also remain unchanged. The way we think and talk about something—the deep, conceptual metaphors we use to explain the world to ourselves—is wired into our brains (Lakoff, 2012, 2014; Hebb, 1949). These metaphors affect what we perceive, how we view learners, the ways we act, and, ultimately, how we teach. To truly change our teaching, we must also change our discourse.

Which brings us to this book, *Made For Learning*. Like my first book, this title took a long time to emerge. Like my first book, the title *Made For Learning* is intended to be a clever contextual pun that reflects the competing theories of literacy learning being hotly debated now. However, this time, the title resulted from a long period of collaborative discussion with my coauthor, Debra Crouch. After reviewing a wide range of research from multiple discipline areas, we identified the core belief, the axiomatic assumption underpinning how we believed classrooms should be organized to ensure that effective, uncomplicated, and durable learning can occur. It was this: As a species, we've been designed to construct and share complex knowledge using symbols. We're the only species on Earth that is capable of doing this. We can't help it. We have literally been "*Made for Learning*."

In this book, Debra Crouch and I set out to help teachers understand what this fundamental assumption means for teaching and learning. To achieve this, we offer a path to changing the inner dialogue of teachers—from a Discourse of

Acquisition to a Discourse of Meaning-Making. What I now believe was missing from *The Whole Story* was an understanding that, as well as changing our theory of learning, we must also consciously change our discourse about learning, teaching, and assessment. In addition, we must ensure our students learn to use a new discourse to think about their work. The work of a learner—in literacy or math or science or history—is, quite simply, making meaning. The discourse of classrooms must reflect this belief.

Dr. Brian Cambourne
University of Wollongong, NSW, Australia
2020

Debra's Story

As I began my teaching career in 1989, Pam Reed, my friend and colleague, and I discovered *The Whole Story*, Brian Cambourne's first book describing the Conditions of Learning. We spent many evenings and weekends reading and talking together about the ideas in the book and how they might play out in our classrooms. Unbeknownst to me at the time, this was the beginning of a journey, one of discovering and articulating my true purpose in a classroom.

While my college degree and state certificate called out *teaching* as my profession, over time, I came to realize this wasn't a complete representation of my work. Yes, I was a teacher in charge of a group of students. Yes, I structured my class to get the kids to do what I wanted them to do (most of the time!), which was basically what the units and teacher's guides said. But, if someone had come into my classroom and actually asked me to describe how you teach someone to read, I'd have been hard pressed to do so.

So, confession: I became a professional development junkie. I'd venture from one professional development *thing* to another, each time, heading back to my own classroom, attempting to implement what I'd heard. I'd try something out, reflect on what I'd tried, and then make adjustments. And, soon, I'd head off to the next professional development session being offered, looking for *answers*. I made the mistakes we all make—too much of this, too little of that. As I practiced, though, and kept talking with colleagues, one line of thinking kept resurfacing and resonating no matter what new idea I tried—the Conditions of Learning.

Over time and through discussions, I began to appreciate the distinction between *teaching* and *helping someone learn*. And this line of thinking mattered tremendously. When the focus of my thinking was *teaching*, I thought first about what I would be doing in a lesson. My decisions led to less-than-productive practices: overreliance on teacher's guides, telling-as-teaching, rewarding compliance and regurgitation of information, and rigid structures.

When *learning* led my thinking, my decisions became more learner-centered. I was guided by questions such as these: How do I support students to value and love learning? How do I build off of the curiosity and joy that accompanies a love of learning? What do my learners need from me in order to see themselves as capable and agentive? How do I design an environment to support this kind of learning? Once these questions emerged, my definition of myself as Teacher shifted. In a learning-centered classroom, I was, among other things, Kidwatcher, Designer, Facilitator, Guide, Coach, Fellow Learner.

Once this role and purpose emerged, I taught differently. Because, when instruction begins from a different perspective, one where we see children as *made for learning*, as our title says, we think, talk, and proceed in very different ways.

My self-talk began to sound something like this: *Oh, if I have the kids read and write every day, that will give them lots of time to* **approximate**..., and, *Hmm, my* **responses** *should help the kids know what they're doing well and what else is possible...* (two of the eight Conditions are in bold, in case you aren't familiar with them yet; two more are below). The Conditions even found their way into my parent sessions as I'd talk with moms and dads (and grandparents and others) about how my work was building on what they, their child's first teachers, had already started. Noting the parent's **expectations** ("Of course I knew they'd learn to talk.") and the children's **employment** ("They never stop talking!") resonated with these caregivers. Over time, my work became more consistent and more firmly grounded in this theory of learning.

In 1993, I was fortunate to visit Sherryl Compston's classroom at Mangere Bridge School in Auckland, New Zealand. Here, I experienced for myself how learner-centered practices flowed and grew. Sherryl shared the tools and structures and, most importantly, the attitudes that brought the Conditions to life. Another professional book came along that helped me understand how to further connect my practices and my beliefs, *Joyful Learning in Kindergarten* by Bobbi Fisher (1991). Bobbi, also a Cambourne follower, helped me learn to notice reading and writing behaviors on a continuum and to make Shared Reading and Shared Writing a central part of my reading, writing, and phonics instruction.

Today, I continue to align my beliefs and practices. As a full-time consultant, I work with educators across the United States as they strive to align their own beliefs and practices. In 2017, my colleagues Pat Eastman, Executive Director for Professional Development at Okapi Educational Publishing, and Cherissa Kreider-Beck, English Language Arts Coordinator at the San Diego County Office of Education, and I designed our first annual literacy conference to support educators. For the three of us, Cambourne's Conditions of Learning remain an underlying theory for learning and teaching. While many teachers we work with are aware of Gradual Release of Responsibility, fewer are aware of Conditions of Learning. And what we were experiencing in classrooms is a rigid application of Gradual Release. For example, some classrooms designate times as "I do," where students take a passive observer role. We believe an understanding of Conditions of Learning supports teachers to recognize the active role of the learner in all components of instruction, regardless of the instructional approach.

So, we contacted Brian for assistance, and he encouraged us to write a piece to fit our needs, generously offering to provide feedback on what we wrote. Quickly, before I chickened out, I committed myself to writing a piece about the Conditions that Brian himself would read. Eventually, that piece became a coauthored article. Enter Brian's idea for collaborating on a book, and the result is what you hold now, a collaboration of our latest thinking about learning and teaching.

Over and over, as I work with educators, I hear questions that begin *How long …, How often …, What do I do when…?* There's an old Peanuts cartoon where Sally, Charlie Brown's little sister, excitedly heads off to school. In the last frame, she's sitting at her desk and saying, "Here I am again—still looking for the answers." Sound familiar? For many educators, professional learning is (as it once was for me) a quest for "answers," a chance for someone to give us the "right" or "best" way to teach. But, while Brian and I facetiously ask the question, "Am I doing this right?" in Chapter 1, neither of us believes in "answers."

My hope for readers of this book is that, through understanding the Conditions of Learning—whether it's the first time hearing about them or it's a revisit— educators will consider and reconsider what it is they believe about learning, decide whether and how their practices align with those beliefs, and, ultimately, trust themselves to make decisions that matter for their learners. To decide for themselves: *What is the distinction between learning and teaching?*

Debra Crouch
San Diego, California, USA
2020

"Learning is a much broader category than education."

——David N. Perkins, *Making Learning Whole: How Seven Principles of Teaching Can Transform Education*

Introduction

Teachers are in the business of learning. We set up our classrooms, assess our students, and create our lessons. We select books, form reading groups, and teach students in those groups regularly. We create complex daily schedules packed with readers' (and writers') workshops, guided reading blocks, and independent reading time. We think aloud, make sure to cover all the comprehension strategies, and use sentence stems to get kids talking. We ask higher-level questions, use turn-and-talk strategies, and make sure every student can write a response to a text. And yet, even with our best intentions, we still wonder: "Am I doing this right?"

This question masquerades as a yes/no question. In reality, it meets all the criteria of an "essential question" (McTighe and Wiggins, 2013): one that is recurring, thought-provoking, and intellectually engaging; one whose response requires higher-order thinking; one that sparks additional questions and further inquiry. Essential questions can't be easily answered; they require justification and "will not have a single, final, and correct answer" (McTighe and Wiggins, 2013). In fact, essential questions don't actually generate *answers;* they generate *thinking.* They require all learners to make meaning as they respond to the question under consideration.

Making Effective Teaching Decisions

Effective teaching requires us to think through a daily wash of information, data, and opinion to provide answers, or meanings, to our own essential questions. Diverse voices from educators (as well as noneducators) talk and write, post and tweet, and blog and share about what to do, say, and think about our learners, often leaving us overwhelmed with choices as to what is truly important and what is just, quite simply, noise.

This book proposes ideas to explore and consider, poses questions to ponder and study, and offers a philosophical viewpoint to reflect on and discuss. Throughout the book, we offer our beliefs about learning and accompanying suggestions on instruction to support educators in their attempts to cut through the noise and clutter and language found in the educational world of today to make decisions that matter for the students in their charge. We offer readers opportunities to consider instructional language and its effects on learning. As our readers shift and focus their awareness on the conceptual metaphors that are wired into our brains, we support a transition from a Discourse of Acquisition to a Discourse of Meaning-Making (Cambourne, 2017).

This book presents a theory of learning known as the Conditions of Learning, describing a lens through which to view the emotional, social, physical, and intellectual settings in which learning is expected. It also describes what we refer to as Processes That Empower Learning, a collection of teaching and learning behaviors that arise when the Conditions are implemented. While many professional conversations and texts about teaching stress the *how* and *what* of instruction, this book is intentionally designed to support teachers to question the *why* of our own beliefs and practices. Why do we do things in the way we do them? This book provides opportunities to consider for *yourself* how and why learning occurs and how to nurture it.

The Design of This Book

Throughout the book are examples of learning and teaching where we believe teacher practices are bringing the Conditions of Learning and the Processes That Empower Learning to life. While the classroom vignettes may be from specific grades, and many are literacy-based, the principles that underlie the exemplary instruction put forth are not grade-or subject-specific.

In Chapter 2, "Theories of Learning and Teaching," we share our theory for how we believe learning occurs as well as what we believe might get in the way of learning. We begin our exploration of what we term a Discourse of Acquisition and a Discourse of Meaning-Making. We are constructivists and believe that learners construct, deconstruct, and reconstruct meanings for themselves. A teacher's role is to support that meaning-making, not to transfer the teacher's knowledge to the learner. Teaching, we feel, is a response to a learner, not a starting point.

> *Teaching is a response to a learner, not a starting point.*

In this second chapter, we begin to share examples of some missteps of instruction, what we refer to as "mismatches" (these continue to occur throughout subsequent chapters). We believe these missteps of instruction are instances of a mismatch between theories of learning and instructional practices employed. As educators, we want to support our readers to identify and consider mismatches in their own practice, to think and discuss mismatches between their belief systems and their own teaching decisions. These mismatches are often hard to recognize in one's own practice. As we describe instructional moments, spaces, structures, or language we see as mismatches, you may see yourself in some of them. (We certainly did!) The intent is not to illuminate our faults and failings but to condition ourselves to be mindful, sensitive, and insightful as we work to be our best teaching selves and reframe the patterns of our discourse. Chapter 2 and subsequent chapters also include text boxes, called "More to the Story," that provide related background for the concepts under discussion.

In addition, in Chapter 2, we introduce a feature called "Thinking about Our Own Meaning-Making." This feature appears throughout Chapters 2–8. We offer this opportunity to take a cognitive breath during reading, to pause and reflect on the specific ideas just discussed in relation to your own practice. At the end of each chapter, the questions are written to support synthesizing the chapter for yourself and then, if possible, engaging in discussion and collaboration with fellow educators about the chapter's big ideas.

Chapter 3, "Introduction to the Conditions of Learning," presents the theory of learning Brian articulated in his earliest research and wrote about in *The Whole Story* (1988). It also expounds his latest thinking about processes that arise in classrooms using the Conditions of Learning as a framework for thinking about learning and teaching. A graphic detailing the Conditions and Processes provides a quick snapshot, illuminating the relationships among these key components that affect a learning situation. Portions of this visual reappear at the beginning of subsequent chapters to remind readers of the relationship of individual Conditions and Processes to the bigger context of a learning setting.

While there is no order of importance or sequence to the Conditions, there is a rationale for the order in which we discuss them. We begin with the Conditions of Immersion and Demonstration. Together, these two Conditions provide the context for what is to be learned. Next, we discuss Engagement, an active stance taken by a learner toward what is being learned. The Conditions of Expectation, Responsibility, Approximation, Employment, and Response concern the interactions of the learner with what is being learned and with the various participants in the learning environment. Each one of these Conditions supports deeper engagement. Each of the Processes That Empower Learning is present in classrooms where the Conditions are intentionally developed and represent interactions among the teacher, the learners, and the content.

Chapters 4–6 offer further detail about each of the Conditions of Learning.

Classroom vignettes illustrate instruction viewed through the lens of the Conditions of Learning. We begin our exploration of individual Conditions with Immersion and Demonstration in Chapter 4, because learning doesn't begin to occur without a learner first experiencing these two Conditions. In Chapter 5, we explore Engagement, a crucial factor in learning and a necessary accompaniment to the immersive and demonstrated learning experiences. Chapter 6 gives context to five Conditions that increase the probability of Engagement: Expectation, Responsibility, Employment, Approximation, and Response.

In Chapter 7, we explore some additional theoretical ideas, which are critical if the Conditions and Processes are to be fully realized. Language, its use, and its development permeate effective instructional settings. We examine M.A.K. Halliday's (1973) theory of simultaneous language development and use inherent in classrooms where the Conditions and Processes exist. His idea of "simultaneousness" is critical to our understandings. Language development and use serve as a bridge between learning and teaching, between the Conditions and the Processes.

When teachers intentionally utilize the Conditions of Learning—in a learning setting built on constructivist principles and simultaneous language development and use—a set of Processes emerges. Chapter 8 explores "Processes That Empower Learning." Transformation, Discussion/Reflection, Application, and Evaluation are all teaching processes that underlie instruction harnessing the potential inherent in the Conditions of Learning.

Our final chapter, Chapter 9, "Using This Theory of Learning to Guide Your Own Practice," is designed to help readers apply this theory of learning to their own practice. In the appendix, we offer templates structured to consider how the Conditions of Learning and Processes That Empower Learning are affected by teaching decisions. Our hope is that readers will recognize the power of teachers to influence the learning possibilities through their own decisions within their own classrooms for their own learners.

Throughout these chapters, each of these Conditions of Learning and Processes That Empower Learning is discussed separately. The most important concept to keep in mind with these Conditions, however, is that they don't have boundaries in a learning setting. Each and every Condition and Process influences and is, in turn, influenced by the others. The Conditions and Processes are interrelated and function holistically. They are synergistic in nature, meaning that, when they are considered together, the total effect is greater than the sum of the individual parts. These Conditions and Processes are inherent in classrooms in which learners are encouraged to use reading, writing, speaking, and listening to explore and make sense of their world.

We believe it's time for educators to rethink what it is we truly believe about learning and why and how it happens (or doesn't happen). Shifting our discourse to one of meaning-making becomes necessary. This shift redefines teaching as a response to learners. It solidifies what we know and want for our learners and revisits the basis for why the kind of teaching we are striving for in our classrooms matters to our learners. This book may be the first step on your journey.

"I need the intense preoccupation of a group of children and teachers inventing new worlds as they learn to know each other's dreams. To invent is to come alive. Even more than the unexamined classroom, I resist the uninvented classroom."
———Vivian Gussin Paley, *The Girl with the Brown Crayon: How Children Use Stories to Shape Their Lives*

Chapter 2

Theories of Learning and Teaching

Effective teaching requires us be the thinkers we want our learners to be—curious, aware, considerate, industrious, interpretive, affirmative, and, yes, inventive. Being this kind of thoughtful teacher enables us to parse through the gimmicks, fads, and cute acronyms to find the heart of what is essential for our children and their learning. Being this kind of teacher necessitates the ability to imagine a place where learning occurs on a consistent basis for all students. To envision and invent this place requires a well-articulated belief system to bring it to life.

A teacher's belief system affects just about everything a teacher does, from how time, space, and resources are bought, organized, and used to the behaviors and routines accepted or rejected for operating the classroom. It guides the teacher's talk and responses to students' attempts, the responses to mistakes, the reprimands or encouragement offered, and so on. If we are ever to provide an "answer" each time we ask, "Am I doing this right?" articulating our own beliefs about how learning happens and our own role in that learning experience is crucial.

What Does It Mean to Learn?

Frank Smith (1983) said, "Metaphors are the legs of language on which thought steadily advances or makes its more daring leaps. Without metaphor thought is inert, and with the wrong metaphor it is hobbled." While we often hear about metaphors as a figure of speech, here the term is used quite differently. Our conceptual metaphors, or mental representations, guide how we think about the world. As educators, our conceptual metaphors affect how we view the purpose of our instruction and the ways we go about our interactions with students, and influence the ways we interpret what we think, see, and hear as we go about teaching. Some familiar conceptual metaphors in education include viewing the child as a flower in a garden to be nurtured, and viewing children as empty vessels to be filled with knowledge.

Even neuroscientists (Cobb, 2020) are grappling with a commonly used meaphor in the field of brain research. Many neuroscientists use a computer as a metaphor as they design studies of the brain. The computer metaphor causes researchers to view the input, or stimuli, and the parts of the brain that activate from those stimuli as the focus of their work. This metaphor influences how they design their experiments and research and how they interpret their findings. Many neuroscientists (Cobb, 2020; Buzsaki, 2019; Fregnac, 2017), however, have begun to view the computer metaphor as limiting, guiding them to continue focusing their research on the components of stimuli and of the regions of the brain that control particular functions. This computer metaphor, these researchers say, may prevent fully understanding the brain's processing capabilities. Many are beginning to "grasp that new analogies could alter how they understand their work" (Cobb, 2020), allowing them to construct new frameworks for understanding *how* the brain makes meaning of the stimuli it receives and forms cognitive networks.

As educators, the conceptual metaphors, or mental representations, we use may limit our understandings and possibilities in this same way. Our mental metaphors directly affect how we view our learners and the processes of learning, teaching, and assessment. When our metaphor views learning as a thing we do or as "stuff" that can be measured and weighed as though it has mass, weight, and heft, we use a mental metaphor that brings forth a collection of teaching and assessment practices that do nothing to advance learning. This view of learning as stuff and learners as vessels to be filled promotes a transmission mode of delivery and is embedded in what we call a Discourse of Acquisition.

Learning, in our view, is our ever-changing knowledge, understandings, feelings, values, and skills regarding what is to be learned. We believe meaning-making *is* learning. Everything a human has ever learned is a sum total of the meanings they have constructed, deconstructed, and reconstructed. By reframing learning as a process of constructing meaning, rather than viewing meaning, or knowledge, as something that exists statically, we create a new conceptual metaphor. The conceptual metaphor underpinning this new frame is that [knowledge-building is a continuous process involving human meaning-making, using abstract symbol systems such as oral and written language (as well as art, drawing, music, etc.). This vision of learning and teaching reflects a Discourse of Meaning-Making (Cambourne, 2017).]

Learning, in our view, is our ever-changing knowledge, understandings, feelings, values, and skills regarding what is to be learned.

Thinking about Our Own Meaning-Making
• How do you define learning?

What Do We Mean by Discourse?

Discourse in common, everyday usage is seen as a synonym for conversation or talk—a sophisticated word choice with a simple meaning. In the world of theoretical, or academic, linguistics, however, Discourse—with a capital D—has a very specific definition. When academic linguists use the term Discourse, they refer to more than just talk, conversation, or other verbal utterances. Discourse, in academia, is a theory of the varied relationships within a particular setting, referring to the ways of thinking and behaving that members of a group expect others to adopt and use when engaged in whatever the group's "business" happens to be. These ways of thinking and behaving include language that reflects a group's values and beliefs. Related to the classroom, then, Discourse would include thinking, behaving, and language use reflecting how literacy classrooms, in particular, and classrooms, in general, should "work."

In our thinking, language refers to any set of abstract symbols used to construct and share meanings. These symbols can be *patterns of sound* (as in the oral language we learn as children or the whistling languages developed by some communities), *patterns of visual symbols* (as in written language, art, sculpture, mathematical formulas, etc.), or *patterns of movements* (as in dance, sign language, gesture, facial expression, mime, etc.). In the real world, some of these systems are used at the same time, as when we use hand movements, gestures, or facial expressions to accompany the sounds we're uttering.

In this way of thinking, therefore, Discourse includes not only particular words and phrases used by participants as they communicate, interact, and respond but also any actions and behaviors, artifacts and tools, and beliefs and understandings that accompany that language. Discourse may include dialect, postures, gestures, facial expressions, tattoos, choice of clothing, rituals, and so on. For example, if we think about the Discourse associated with a church setting, it involves not only the language used but the rituals and routines, the dress and mannerisms, and the beliefs and canons of a particular religion, all of which are held together through the verbal language being used by the members of that specific religion being practiced. In a sense, the language used in such settings is like the glue that holds it together. Another familiar example is found at sporting events; the same principles of Discourse apply as fans tailgate with particular food and drink, don specific player's jerseys for game day, and recite insider knowledge of team dynamics and player stats. All these ways of thinking and behaving and talking are understood, accepted, and encouraged by fans of whatever team is followed.

Discourse in a classroom is no different. The same range of elements—words and phrases, actions and behaviors, artifacts and tools, and beliefs and understandings—identifies it as such: raising hands and walking in the hallways, desks and chalk or white boards, books and paper and pencils, questions and answers, and teachers and students. The Discourse within any particular classroom, however, will vary; that variation is what invokes the sense and sensibilities for the learners. The arrangement of seating, the use of texts and other resources, and the interactions and language used by the members—the Discourse—will differ from classroom to classroom. These differing Discourses can make learning, for learners, sensible or senseless, abundantly thoughtful or complicated, fertile and productive, or seemingly disconnected.

In a classroom, the Discourse can be one of Acquisition or one of Meaning-Making, or it can be a mix of these elements. So, what is the nature of this mix in the classroom? This book explores differences between these Discourses and the teaching decisions we make as we work toward meaning-driven teaching and learning.

Thinking about Our Own Meaning-Making

- Consider your own classroom. What teaching decisions are meaning driven?

- Which aren't?

- How might you adjust those decisions to make them meaning-driven?

What Is Meaning-Making?

This shift from a Discourse of Acquisition to a Discourse of Meaning-Making invokes quite a different way of thinking about knowledge and the processes of learning and teaching. Instead of a discourse that subconsciously implies that learning is the process of moving stuff from one place (e.g., an expert's mind, a book, or a film) to a learner's mind by an act of transmission (using language as the medium), a Discourse of Meaning-Making frames learning as a process of using linguistic and other symbols to engage in continuous cycles of constructing, deconstructing, and reconstructing these meanings in interaction with others. In other words, we construct meaning using all the texts that exist in whatever medium is available to us—print, graphic, oral, sign, gestures, etc.—as we think and talk alongside other learners. These meanings are continually being adjusted and updated as we learn more; learning doesn't stop when we close a book or finish a conversation. When it comes to literacy, learning is our ever-changing knowledge, understandings, feelings, values, and skills about literacy, literacy learning, and literacy use.

More to the Story
Other Professional Thinking That Exemplifies the Discourse of Meaning-Making

We see the Discourse of Meaning-Making (Cambourne, 2017) inherent in the work of other scholars. M.A.K. Halliday (1973) was one of the first to recognize that we "learn language, learn through language, and learn about language *simultaneously.*" Another pioneer in this field is James Britton (1970). He spoke of reading and writing floating on a sea of talk, linking these often-viewed silos of practice. Frank Smith reiterated these ideas when he wrote that we "learn to read by reading" and learn to write by "reading like a writer" (1983), recognizing the need for teachers to use meaningful texts as a platform for learning. When Richard Allington (2006) named "thoughtful literacy" as a necessary factor for struggling reader's success, he detailed meaning-making as central to all learning. In his theory of talk existing on a continuum, Douglas Barnes (2008) linked language to the construction of meaning. Peter Johnston (2012) discussed how language changes children's lives and asked us to rephrase our teaching language to support a dynamic learning frame. In her work, Maria Nichols (2019a) offered examples of facilitative language for teachers as they support children to use purposeful talk as a meaning-making tool.

All these educators, past and present, believe meaning-making is central to all learning. Each offers professional language intended to alter a teacher's thinking and bring about a different teaching dynamic within a classroom. We, too, believe different language supports a different Discourse, one which uncomplicates and recenters our focus on learning and meaning-making. Throughout this book, we articulate a particular Discourse—the Discourse of Meaning-Making—and the actions and behaviors, artifacts and tools, and beliefs and understandings that accompany this theory of learning.

Mismatches between Theory and Practice

A belief system, a perspective, and a philosophy, are, in fact, synonyms for a theory. Earlier, in Chapter 1, we voiced a question many teachers ask: "Am I doing this right?" Our experience of and data from observing and interviewing teachers and students in classrooms strongly suggest where this question originates. An inability to evaluate our own teaching decisions and practices for ourselves often stems from a mismatch in philosophies (i.e., belief systems or theories) about learning and the teaching decisions we've made. It's problematic when the theory to which you ascribe and the practices you're attempting to implement are incongruent. It's also challenging to evaluate your own teaching decisions when you lack a cohesive theory from which to reason. When we haven't had the opportunity to explore and discuss our beliefs about what effective learning actually involves or looks and sounds like in action, we tend to have a confused and incomplete understanding of what learning "is" or how to match good learning theory with effective classroom practices.

Mismatches between theory and practices often surface and manifest in the language we use in our interactions with our learners. Our beliefs about learning are reflected in our language choices, regardless of our stated philosophies or chosen instructional practices; our old Discourse forces us to behave in certain ways. For example, a teacher may say to students, "When you finish your work, you will have time to read your book." This language positions "reading your book" as something less important than whatever reading-related tasks the teacher has deemed "work." Those who complete the tasks and "get to read" may come to see reading as a filler, while those who don't manage to finish those tasks may be denied the opportunity to engage in sustained reading at all. Our language reveals more about us to others, especially children, than we may realize. Our language and interactions can have "profound effects on children's development" and "influence who they think they are and what they think they're doing" (Johnston, 2012).

Another example common in classrooms today is to talk about "mistakes" being a sign of learning (which they are). To encourage growth mindsets (Dweck, 2006), teachers may typically encourage children to be okay with mistakes. In literacy lessons, teachers may talk about students making "mistakes" or "errors" when they read and may offer fix-up strategies for when that happens. In math lessons, "mistakes" are now expected in discussions of problem-solving. Regardless of how often a teacher may repeat, "Mistakes are signs of learning" or "It's okay to make mistakes in our classroom," if a learner's "accuracy" or "answer" is judged and graded, or used to determine placement in groups or to identify what books or activities are made available, "mistakes" are not truly valued as a sign of learning. This is a mismatch between what teachers say they want students to do and what teachers end up doing with the ideas presented by the learners as they actively engage in their learning process. This is an example of a mismatch between the language we use and the actions we take that undermines the trusting relationship between a child and teacher. It also can undermine the student's belief in himself or herself as a learner. The results of mismatches such as these can be momentous, as they directly affect student engagement.

Mismatches in instructional language can also arise from incomplete or inaccurate knowledge in the subject areas in which we teach, such as when we share literacy strategies that don't reflect what literate people actually do. One

[handwritten margin note: So true!]

regular occurrence in a primary classroom involves the teacher telling students what to do when they come to an unknown word: "Sound it out." Letter-by-letter decoding of a word is a necessary ability for a reader to possess. Letter-by-letter decoding, however, isn't the strategy a skilled reader uses *first* upon encountering a problem in reading; effective readers tend to look for patterns of letters. When letter-by-letter decoding is the primary, or only, strategy prompted by a teacher, children fail to develop a repertoire of strategies for problem-solving words.

Mismatch between Theory and Practice
Teaching Readers to "Sound It Out"

Readers read with "divided attention," focusing on the meaning of a text being read while simultaneously paying attention to the print, or visual information (Fountas and Pinnell, 1996, 2006, 2007, 2016b; Burkins and Croft, 2010; Clay, 1991). This divided attention leads the reader to problem-solve new words using "redundancy" in text (i.e., using multiple ways of knowing, such as looking at illustrations for meaning, rereading sentences to access the language cues in the sentences, and checking letters and letter patterns) (Holdaway, 1979; Smith, 1978). Readers use as much visual information, or print, as needed in conjunction with the other sources of information, meaning and structure, to confirm their own reading; letter-by-letter decoding is a last resort. As readers reread, they may repeat the sentence or phrase up to the problem word and then make the first sound of the unknown word. When more visual information than initial letters is needed, effective readers use the largest parts of a word possible (i.e., letter patterns) to speed up the word-solving. Encouraging readers to "sound it out" as an *initial strategy* when they come to problem words, which is typically demonstrated as letter-by-letter decoding, is inefficient teaching that can lead to inefficient reading.

Another example of a mismatch between belief systems and our instructional practices is when we don't "practice what we preach." Nothing creates mistrust as easily and quickly as when students realize teachers don't actually do what they insist students should spend their time doing. And this mistrust undermines the engagement that is central to all learning. Donalyn Miller (2009), in *The Book Whisperer: Awakening the Inner Reader in Every Child*, says that underneath all good instruction is "a child reading a book." But there is more to Miller's story than just providing children with books. The children in her classroom are being led by a teacher who is herself a lifelong reader; she is a teacher who builds, maintains, and encourages a community whose members (including herself) share a passion: reading! Teachers like Miller think, talk, and interact differently with students than do teachers who lack the passion that reading inspires.

Katie Wood Ray (2001) echoes this same belief about teachers of writers. Ray reflects that the "tone of the teaching in a room where the students know their teachers as writers will always be different than the tone in rooms where the students know their teachers as people who ask them to do something that they don't actually do themselves." This tone, the soul of the learner—teacher relationship, is what enables a learner to engage with our lesson demonstrations. This engagement makes learning more likely.

Each of these examples reflects a mismatch between a teacher's belief system and the language used in instruction. By this, we mean the patterns of sounds, symbols, and movements and the metaphors we use—our Discourse. In some instances, such as the example of "mistakes," a teacher may go through the motions of constructivist teaching but, actually, at his or her core, believe that acquisition is how we learn. Others may give voice to the tenets of constructivism but practice in ways more aligned with the belief system of acquisition. For example, when teachers use components of holistic instructional models, such as independent libraries, but then choose to organize the books by levels, this reflects a misalignment between philosophy and practice. As we think about learning and teaching, our language—and, therefore, our practice—is often laced with subtle metaphors that stop us from thinking beyond transmission of knowledge. We, in effect, are "prisoners" of a Discourse of Acquisition. Understanding why you do something in the way you do it requires a reflective stance, which makes it possible for you to understand your own decision-making. Aligning our belief system and the language of our discourse (the patterns of sounds, symbols, and movements and the metaphors we use) that accompanies those beliefs is necessary if we truly want our teaching, and, consequently, the learning, to be different.

> ### *Mismatch between Theory and Practice*
> ### Using Levels as a Means of Selecting Books for Independent Reading
>
> If our classroom libraries (those housed within our individual classrooms, where students self-select materials for independent reading) are organized by levels only and we ask students to find "just right" books, the message communicated is that level, whether quantitative (e.g., Lexile) or qualitative (e.g., Fountas and Pinnell), is the way for a student to know whether a book is right for him or her. This is a mismatch between a definition of "just right" and what exists in the real world of reading. When a reader, regardless of age, knows little about a topic, the reader probably needs to begin with an easier text (i.e., a lower level). When a reader knows more about a topic, he or she can read much more complex books on the topic (i.e., a higher level). When readers are highly motivated to read a book because others are reading it or are fascinated by the topic, they will persevere and seek out friends or other sources to help understand the book—just ask any Harry Potter fan! Leveling is helpful, but it was never intended as an overarching organization in terms of student choice of books for reading independently (Fountas and Pinnell, 2017).

> **Thinking about Our Own Meaning-Making**
> • **What mismatches in your own teaching practice can you identify?**

Common-Sense Theories of Learning

Common-sense theories have always existed. They influence our behavior in subtle but significant ways. For example, it was once common sense to believe Earth was flat, and this common sense was so obvious to what the human eye seemed to see every day that no one questioned the assumption. The long-held perception of Earth being flat affected how ships sailed and navigated, striking fear into the hearts of experienced sailors and novices alike. The domain of learning is subject to the same "common-sense" attitudes.

A common-sense theory, or belief system, associated with the domain of learning posits that it starts with teaching, defined as an effort that is applied to a learner. In this belief system, teaching is seen as a mode of delivery, a transfer of knowledge, with knowledge regarded as tangible "stuff"—as though it has mass that can be weighed, measured, and moved around (as we stated earlier). Examples of common-sense teaching and learning present themselves readily in the classroom: circling spelling errors in red pen to show children the words to correct in their writing, telling a writer what she or he should add to make their writing better, or giving all students the same template to follow every time they write. Each of these techniques can get a piece of writing produced, but none actually strengthens the abilities of the writer.

Once this view of knowledge is accepted as common sense, it follows that ideas and information can be given or transferred from one person to another. Our discourse becomes embedded with particular language, such as "today I'm going to teach you...." From this belief and its accompanying discourse, an adult teacher passes on knowledge—ideas and information—to a student, who is less experienced. The learner is a compliant recipient of these ideas and information, until the student is asked to restate the ideas and information the teacher presented as proof of learning. The ideas and information presented as learning are then deemed by the teacher to be right or wrong, complete or incomplete.

In this model of learning, the belief system and related discourse demand that teachers must first "cover" every comprehension strategy and individual skill so that students can succeed. Without that instruction, students won't be successful learners. Within this belief system and related discourse, we assess children to find out what they don't know and what they didn't absorb from instruction. The resulting teaching experiences are ongoing efforts to "fill in the gaps."

In all models of learning, there will be those students for whom learning doesn't happen as readily as it does for others. In this common-sense belief system and related discourse, these learners begin to be assessed more often, using ever more finely detailed, gap-identifying tests, and then receive more attention and time from well-meaning adults who see their purpose as "filling in the gaps" for these students. And while the learner may come to hold on to bits and pieces of the "taught" information, he or she struggles to orchestrate these bits and pieces into bigger ideas and understandings.

This belief system and related discourse consider the teacher's stance first and what the teacher must do *to* and *for* the learner in order for learning to occur. The primary question a teacher asks is, "What do I do to teach the learner?"

A Different Theory of Learning

All children are made for learning. Although some educators debate whether children are "wired" to learn to read and write, we believe all children have the potential to learn. Learning to read and write is part of that all-encompassing potential. Indeed, children have already demonstrated their learning potential by the time they start formal schooling—they have already accomplished "a stunning intellectual achievement" (Cambourne, 1988) by learning a language (or, sometimes, multiple languages simultaneously). And this language (or languages) has developed with the necessary, multilayered complexities and nuances required to communicate effectively with a range of others who speak that language (Halliday, 2003; Tomasello, 2003; Deacon, 1997).

Under the best circumstances, school learning builds on the attitudes, behaviors, and understandings about learning that develop before formal schooling begins; it respects each learner as a learner. Learners are viewed not as empty vessels to be filled with stuff called *school knowledge* but as capable individuals with the potential to construct meanings using symbols, and to communicate and share these meanings with others, usually through oral and written language. Human beings are the only species on Earth with the potential to construct and share complex, abstract meanings, or knowledge, with those meanings primarily constructed and conveyed through oral and written language.

Knowledge, in this theory of learning, is viewed as a creation and outcome of all the meanings constructed by the learner as she or he is learning. Knowledge, or meaning, is thus something a learner constructs, deconstructs, and reconstructs as she or he engages in purposeful interactions with other learners around what is to be learned. And, in the way all creations evolve, this knowledge is dynamic and can be influenced and expanded as new experiences occur.

A Constructivist Belief System

These beliefs and related discourse about learning offer a constructivist view of learning in which learning is viewed as "the process of continually constructing, deconstructing, and reconstructing meanings while interacting and communicating with others (and with oneself) ... using a range of symbols and symbol systems" (Cambourne, 2013). The ability to construct and communicate abstract meaning through symbols accounts for the success of humans as a species; it is also the key trait that ultimately makes humans . . ., well, human.

Many myths surround constructivism and balanced instruction. A constructivist view of learning doesn't favor one instructional approach over another; a constructivist teacher doesn't switch to whatever current iteration of instruction is in vogue. A constructivist viewpoint isn't code for "discover everything on your own." Nor is it a directive to ignore skill instruction. A constructivist viewpoint doesn't advocate making sure our daily schedule includes enough small-group time or times designated as "I do" or "we do." A constructivist view doesn't include a directive to try everything in the educational playbook to achieve a happy medium with "research-based" being the lone belief system to guide us. This isn't what balanced instruction is about.

Instead, a constructivist viewpoint and the related Discourse of Meaning-Making encourages us to create deliberate classroom opportunities that include immersion in and demonstrations of all aspects of literacy or numeracy or science or history. It includes extended times for all learners to approximate, use, and take responsibility for their own learning. It also incorporates times for appropriate responses from the teacher and other students. Expectations, engagement, and collaboration are key ideas for learning. So, "balanced" doesn't mean making choices among practices or achieving a happy middle ground. Balanced pedagogy involves envisioning and implementing intentional and consistent conditions and practices that recognize and honor the human need to make meaning of our world, which includes making sense of these abstract symbols found in texts, and the strong need to communicate that meaning.

Learning about Oral Language

Consider how we usually think about children before they enter the first grade. They struggle to tie their shoes or button their own clothing; they regularly engage in pretend play, sometimes with imaginary friends; they have meltdowns when

> *More to the Story*
> ## Children for Whom Talking Doesn't Develop
>
> There are humans born with intact and functioning nervous systems who sometimes don't learn to talk or have great difficulty doing so. One such example is children for whom deafness occurs before they learn to speak (Sacks, 1989–). Helen Keller is the best-known example of how difficult and confusing it can be for someone to learn oral language when she or he can't be immersed in or can't witness how oral language "sounds" (cadences, rhythms, intonation, etc.) or how it can be used. Teachers of deaf students attest to the challenges these students face in learning to speak; however, learning to communicate through sign language demonstrates their capabilities to make meaning.
>
> There are also examples of abused or neglected children who fail to develop the ability to speak even though they possess the physiological abilities to do so. (Fortunately, the numbers are small for such cases.) In the 1970s, a child who had been confined to a small room under abusive conditions of physical restraint was discovered. The girl, named Genie, had received only minimal human contact from the age of eighteen months to almost fourteen years. She knew no language and was not able to talk, although she subsequently learned some language (Curtiss, 1977). In another tragic situation, the effects of not having a community of user experts to respond to and communicate with is vividly described in Charles A. Nelson's (2007) account of the effects of human deprivation on Romanian orphans.
>
> The existence of such cases suggests that learning to control the oral mode of language might also be contingent on the availability of environmental factors or other conditions. (This is supported by current brain research we discuss in Chapter 7.)

they don't get their way. All these behaviors, and others like them, are accepted as normal because the child is, after all, a child. This immaturity is expected given the child's age. (These same behaviors in an adult, on the other hand, would be frowned upon and considered worrisome.)

While children may be considered immature in many ways, given their ages, by the time they reach the age of six or so, most will have developed the major portions of grammatical structures for the language(s) they speak (Snow, 2009; C. Chomsky, 1976; Labov, 1972). Children (and adults) don't acquire language as though it is something given to them by others. Children (and adults) generalize from language examples they experience (Freeman and Freeman, 2004; Gibbons, 1993; C. Chomsky, 1976). Language learners generate, try out, and accept or reject grammatical rules they have constructed as they communicate and interact with others. This interaction provides the necessary feedback to determine the effectiveness of their communication and adjust their language accordingly. These constructed understandings about a unique, arbitrary set of sounds and rules and how to combine them into a language that can generate complex meaning are truly a stunning intellectual achievement. The fact that children achieve this cognitive ability so quickly and painlessly and universally while being so immature otherwise is breathtaking.

Learning about Written Language

Differences do exist between learning to talk and learning to read; there are different kinds of knowledge to construct about each. For example, in print, word boundaries

More to the Story

Some Similarities and Differences between Oral and Written Language (Pinnell and Fountas, 1998; Gibbons, 1993; Cambourne, 1988; Smith, 1983)

Oral	Written	Both
• Intonation and expression help meaning to be more easily understood.	• Written language is used to record ideas and information so we can remember and communicate them.	• Both are examples of the unique human ability to construct and communicate meaning using different symbol systems.
• Oral language is contextualized and influenced by topic, relationships of speakers, and visual contact (or lack of) between speakers.	• It can be used to hold language and ideas up for reflection and analysis.	• Both are purposeful.
• Gestures add meaning to words used or may convey meaning without words.	• Written language use is designed to communicate across time and space.	• They offer opportunities to figure out what you think.
• Print conventions don't exist in oral language.	• Special features exist in written language such as syntax (dialogue) and punctuation.	• Language in either form is best learned by making sense of what is meant through its perceived use.
• Grammatical intricacies, which are context bound, such as using more pronouns, may be present and occur more frequently.	• Ideas can be manipulated in time and space.	• Contextualized and situational meaningfulness of the words is conveyed by both print (signs) and oral language.
• More understanding may be assumed or communicated with fewer words, or in shorthand, if conversational partners are familiar with each.	• There is increased lexical density within the sentence forms used in some text types.	• Both are used to create experiences and explore ideas.
• It is interactive, in-the-moment, and unpredictable.	• Words and grammatical structures may be different from those used in oral language (i.e., generalizations/ formal language vs. contextualized/informal language).	

exist that aren't readily apparent when we speak. In written texts, we name the speaker of utterances and use quotation marks to delineate what was said. Neither of these understandings exists in oral language. Some would use this argument about differences to bolster and defend a transmission model of teaching. In a transmission model, learners must be given knowledge about what is to be learned from a teacher before it can be used or applied by the learner. There is no allowance or permission to approximate. What is to be learned is an either/or proposition—either you have it or you don't. This is a hallmark of the Discourse of Acquisition.

In a constructivist model of learning, however, learners are given opportunities to use language in purposeful experiences to understand how this puzzle we call language works. In this model, learning about print language through its use offers children time and space in which to construct understandings and generalizations about how print functions and to study how meanings are conveyed through print as opposed to oral language. Teaching about language and its use "might well be directed toward providing a fertile environment in which this natural capacity can flourish" (C. Chomsky, 1976). This fertile environment necessitates reading, thinking, talking, and writing about ideas. The teacher's role becomes one of creating and carefully managing space and time for numerous demonstrations of and references to how language works, both oral and written, in service of meaning. Through speaking and listening and writing and reading about meaningful ideas, we believe children come to recognize the similarities and differences in each form. Because, ultimately, how could learning to control the written form of language be considered any more difficult, complex, or demanding than learning to control the oral form (Cambourne, 1988)?

This learning about language, both oral and written, is a direct consequence of interactions with multiple agents, including the classroom teacher, other adults, and other young learners who serve as models of and gauges for effective language use. Through these interactions, children not only come to understand the components (e.g., letters, sounds, words, punctuation, and genre) necessary to communicate in oral and written form but also develop a keen desire to use those elements in conventional forms. In this way, Halliday's theory of learning, describing learning as a linguistic process for making meaning, comes to life. Learners "learn language, learn through language, and learn about language simultaneously" (Halliday, 1973).

What is to be learned is different. However, the conditions that support that learning are not.

When one considers the existence of *conditions* that increase the likelihood of learning, including learning to speak the language of the culture into which one is born, it stands to reason that other forms of learning, including about written language, should be learned just as readily if those conditions are present. Yes, what is to be learned is different. However, the conditions that support that learning are not.

Thinking about Our Own Meaning-Making

• **What professional resources do you rely upon to support your theory or beliefs about learning?**

Changing One's Belief System

Change isn't easy for most people. Uncertainty can cause us to cling to what we've done in the past, whether it was successful or not, or to focus entirely on organizational structures or time, the easiest components to measure even if these aren't true measures of success.

Changing belief systems compels us to reconsider the language we use to describe our work, to revise our discourse from one of acquisition to one of meaning-making. The phrase "to teach" is often used to describe a teacher's role within a learning experience. This grammatical language structure positions teaching as a verb, and, as a verb, the reference demands an object. You don't just "teach," you teach "someone something." Just using this grammar in our own thinking forces us to subconsciously think of teaching as something a teacher does to a learner. This language articulates a belief about our role in the learning experience, reinforcing the notion that teaching is a delivery system for the transference of some tangible stuff called knowledge or skills, from one place (an expert's mind) to an empty space (a learner's mind).

Changes in any behavior are preceded by changes in thinking (beliefs, values, theories, etc.), and these changes are promoted (or hindered) by linguistic choice. Teaching behaviors are no different. Imagine how our own beliefs and practice could be affected if we replaced the sentence "I am teaching a guided reading lesson" with "I am creating an opportunity for learners to make meaning in a guided reading lesson." What different teaching decisions might we make during the lesson? Or, "Today, we are learning math/science/history…" is replaced with "Today, we will be making meaning as we think like mathematicians/scientists/historians…." How might that change in language affect learners?

By changing our discourse from one of acquisition to one of meaning-making, our teaching "work" becomes not "doing" instructional strategies but "using" instructional strategies to support students to make meaning. It changes from being about "covering" comprehension strategies to being about supporting students to understand how they already have used strategies to make meaning. For students, their reading "work" becomes about "thinking" and "making meaning." With this change in language, in discourse, how might our teaching practices look, sound, and feel different? How might we view our role in learning opportunities? And how might our change in language impact how learners view themselves and their purpose in learning settings? What ultimately becomes possible?

Conclusion

We strive to create classrooms where literacy culminates in "active, critical, productive thinking and problem solving ... which makes it possible for us to successfully negotiate both our school (academic) world and the world outside school" (Cambourne, 1988). In these classrooms, teachers assume responsibility for establishing an intentional learning setting. Essential questions asked by teachers in these classrooms—teachers with a constructivist belief—include "What does this learner know already?" and "How can I support these students to learn more?" These questions do not have easy, tweetable 140- (or 280-) character answers. But ... teachers with constructivist belief systems don't expect them to.

In our next chapter, we introduce the Conditions of Learning that make this constructivist belief system come to life, followed by examples from classrooms that illustrate what it means to hold constructivist beliefs.

Thinking about Our Own Meaning-Making

• **What is your theory of learning? How does the description of learning in this chapter align with your beliefs about learning?**

• **What is an example of a mismatch between your theory of learning and an instructional practice you use or have used? How might you adjust the practice to align with your theory of learning?**

• **What other big ideas are you holding as you reflect on this chapter? What questions do you have?**

"Children do not need to be taught that they can learn. . .
Children believe their brains are all-potent until they learn otherwise."

——Frank Smith, *Essays into Literacy*

Chapter 3

Introduction to the Conditions of Learning

Brian has spent nearly five decades documenting how children learn and teachers teach in "natural settings." This chapter outlines his framework known as the Conditions of Learning.

From 1972 to 1988, Brian observed, recorded, documented, and analyzed the ebb and flow of language use in home, school, and classroom settings to identify how learning to talk occurred so successfully, easily, and painlessly. From the data compiled, he identified certain conditions that make this complex learning possible, and, from 1988 to 2017, he invited teachers to turn the conditions he identified into classroom practice as he and his colleagues observed, documented, and analyzed that instruction, called literacy. As Brian noted in his story that prefaces this book, he has come to believe that one of the barriers to developing a classroom based on his research findings is the language we use in our instructional settings and the language we use to describe the purpose of our work. Our discourse, used in both reflection and discussion, greatly impacts the instructional decisions we make. This mismatch in our beliefs and our discourse also communicates mixed messages to the students we teach regarding their purpose in the classroom.

Why Naturalistic Inquiry?

In naturalistic inquiry, researchers conduct their work in a natural setting. This research is designed and conducted differently from experimental research, which uses control groups. (The latter is designed specifically to test a predetermined hypothesis or to determine a cause–effect relationship.) In a natural setting, the setting has not been deliberately contrived by a researcher. This big difference between naturalistic inquiry and experimental research hinges on the fact that the naturalistic inquiry researcher has little or no control over what those being observed will say or do or how they'll respond to what happens. Because of this lack of control, researchers describe these settings as "experimenter-free."

Naturalistic inquiry researchers are motivated to understand how complex systems such as home and classroom settings work. Unlike experimental researchers, Brian was not interested in establishing cause-and-effect relationships; he, instead, sought to understand underlying patterns and systems that effectively support durable learning. The Conditions of Learning offer both a theoretical and a practical framework for redefining and reframing the notion of a balanced pedagogy.

Biomimicry and the Conditions of Learning

Brian continues to write and speak on the topic of learning as he incorporates current research about biomimicry into his thinking. In his latest work, he considers whether nature has already developed pedagogy for learning to read and asks us to apply the ecological, social, physical, and emotional conditions that support learning to talk to learning to read (Cambourne, 2013).

Scientists, engineers, and designers in a relatively new field of scientific endeavor called *biomimicry* ask us to learn from and then emulate the intelligence embedded in 3.8 billion years of learning, using nature's forms, processes, and ecosystems to create more sustainable designs (Biomimicry Institute, 2020). Biomimicry represents an approach to science that focuses on "the science and art of emulating Nature's best biological ideas to solve human problems."

From fishing nets mimicking spiderwebs to snowshoes designed like the feet of snowshoe hares to Velcro using hooked burrs like those found on burdock seeds, when faced with a problem or issue, biomimicry's researchers ask, "How would nature solve this?" or "Has nature solved this already?" These innovators look to the natural world for models and mentors, seeking to learn from nature's playbook. With applications from da Vinci to the Wright Brothers to NASA, biomimicry's designs are based on phenomena that are observed in nature.

As an educator who has spent fifty years trying to develop an educationally relevant, ecologically valid theory of learning (Cambourne, 1972, 1988, 1995, 2001, 2013, 2017), Brian has explored biomimicry and reaped new insights to bring to this quest (Cambourne, 2007). Rather than thinking like a social scientist, Brian has begun thinking like a biologist.

Biologists argue that what distinguishes *Homo sapiens* from all other forms of life on our planet are two unique cognitive abilities: 1) creating complex knowledge (or "meanings") using abstract symbol systems and 2) applying this knowledge (or these "meanings") to the everyday problems of the survival of a species (like humans learning to read and write critically in a democracy!). And, not only are we the only species of living organisms on the planet that can construct abstract meanings using a diverse range of symbol systems, but we can store these meanings in memory. This gives us the ability to revisit them, manipulate them, extend them, refine them, build on them—and then share and communicate what we've constructed as consequences of all these processes with other members of the species.

These cognitive abilities that characterize only our species strongly suggest that nature has already worked out what social, cultural, and physical factors are needed to make such complex learning possible. Psychology and other social sciences frame learning as a change in behavior and seek to measure that change, whereas biology frames learning and knowledge as the *end product of a process of meaning-making using abstract symbol systems*. Learning is seen as a special way of knowing. Brian's research into the conditions that make this learning, this meaning-making, more likely to occur aligns with nature's playbook.

Why Study Learning to Talk?

In 1988, in *The Whole Story: Natural Learning and the Acquisition of Literacy in the Classroom,* Brian offered educators (including Debra, coauthor of this book) a different way of thinking about learning and teaching, a departure from "common-sense" instructional approaches (as we discussed in Chapter 2) at a time that focused primarily on the teacher's role in learning. His research into conditions in which we successfully learn to talk—coupled with the notion that oral and written forms of language are "parallel manifestations of the mind's effort to create meaning"—detailed a powerful view of literacy learning that has come to be known as the Conditions of Learning.

By studying children who are learning to talk, Brian's research examines one of the most universal examples of complex learning in which humans engage. It's universal because all cultures have languages that must be learned by all newborn members, irrespective of class, socioeconomic setting, social status, family structure, and home environment. Furthermore, although most cognitive scientists and/or linguists regard learning to talk as the most complex learning task humans ever face—and because it occurs so regularly and so successfully—we often take the process for granted.

Thinking about Our Own Meaning-Making
• **Have you ever observed a child learning to talk? What interested, intrigued, or fascinated you about this process?**

To date, Brian has identified eight Conditions of Learning and four Processes That Empower Learning. His initial research included observing young children in their home environments as they learned to speak their native languages and identifying patterns of factors (forces/principles/conditions) that seemed to support this learning. He then asked teachers to design purposeful literacy learning settings that were supported by these factors, or conditions, at the classroom level. He and the teachers next observed what happened. Over years of observations, the Processes That Empower Learning have emerged as the kinds of interactions, or teaching behaviors, that result from applying the Conditions, which, in turn, strengthen the overall impact of the Conditions.

Cambourne's Model of Learning

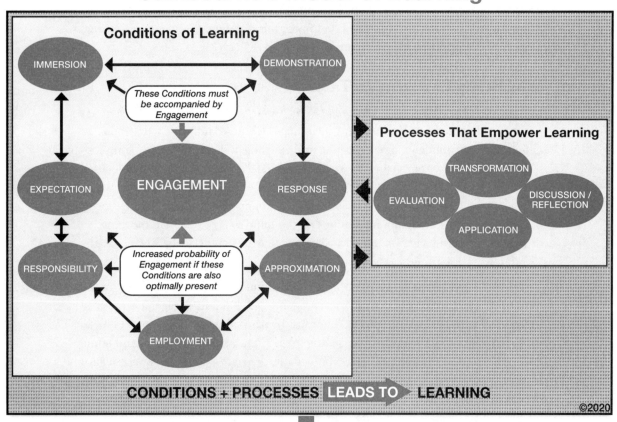

What Are the Conditions of Learning?

What follows is a brief description of the Conditions. While each Condition is described separately, they function synergistically and holistically in practice.

Each Condition is defined in this chapter and more fully articulated and illustrated by classroom examples in the ensuing chapters. Immersion and Demonstration are discussed in Chapter 4. Engagement is examined in Chapter 5. The Conditions of Expectation, Responsibility, Employment, Approximation, and Response are explored in Chapter 6.

Immersion

Immersion is when someone witnesses a visual and/or aural experience of what is being learned. These contextualized experiences can be teacher-controlled or learner-controlled, or even incidental, examples of what is being learned. Immersive experiences support a learner in understanding the full effects of what is being learned with all the physical, social, emotional, and intellectual aspects present. Immersive experiences help learners identify how different aspects (both visible and nonvisible, conscious and unconscious) of things being witnessed *might* be connected, related, and categorized. Often, the aspects novice learners identify lead to immature or incomplete approximations or "theories of the world." Common examples of these approximations include baby talk, using the pictures only to read a story, and inventing spelling when writing. These approximations ultimately change as more immersion, demonstrations, and responses occur and novices begin to understand and use the culturally appropriate and more sophisticated forms. As indicated above, these immersive events are a complex mix of physical, social, emotional, and intellectual factors.

Demonstration

A demonstration involves artifacts and/or actions that provide multiple opportunities to recognize and appreciate, know and understand, and act and apply certain skills, behaviors, and "know-how" in the world. All learning begins when one engages with a demonstration of some kind. The goal of a demonstration is for learners to witness and engage in the processes of what is being learned and, over time, work out how to apply the skills and knowledge embedded in the demonstration and, ultimately, become able to apply the learning for themselves in other situations.

Just as with immersion, the most powerful demonstrations of learning begin with "wholes" of knowledge or behavior. In other words, these powerful demonstrations are holistically experienced first before the parts are explored. Demonstrations such as these support a learner in understanding how the component parts and processes of a learning experience are orchestrated into a meaningful, whole artifact or action.

Engagement

Engagement is a participatory stance taken by a learner about what is being demonstrated. This Condition is at the center of all learning. For learning to occur, a learner must engage with any demonstration in which they are immersed. Without engagement, even the clearest and best-designed demonstration isn't likely to result in learning.

Engagement is more likely to occur if learners see themselves as "doers" of the behavior in which they are immersed; if they understand how demonstrations are important to their lives; if they believe they aren't risking physical or psychological harm by attempting the behavior; and if they like, trust, respect, and want to emulate the person demonstrating. These four principles must be embedded in the discourse and ethos of the classroom setting and culture the teacher wants to create.

Expectation

Expectations involve beliefs about learners' capabilities, both how learners view themselves and how they are viewed by significant others. As described in the section on Engagement, learners must see themselves as being capable of learning.

Often, this belief, or sense of self, is signaled through the messages and language significant others use when communicating with learners. When parents are asked whether they expect their children to learn to talk, their response is an unqualified "Yes." But, when asked whether their child will learn to read, their response is more conditional: "I hope so" or "If they get a good teacher." These messages communicate very different beliefs about a learner's capabilities and can dramatically affect his or her sense of self as a learner.

Responsibility

Independent learners are learners who know how to make learning decisions about what, when, and how they will learn. Dependent learners rely on others to tell them what to learn and how to learn it. Only truly independent learners can be responsible for what they will take from demonstrations and when they will take anything.

While learning to talk, learners decide what part or parts of a demonstration they attend to and when they will attend to a particular language task. For example, consider a language demonstration in the form of a command: "Please put on your shoes." The learner may be noticing the idea of "shoes" and what they are, or the way to include the word *please* when making a request. Alternatively, the learner may be considering the context of the message, as in, "When I put on my shoes, it's time to go outside." When learning to write, learners choose when to use a word wall to check the spelling of words rather than ask an adult for spellings. Ultimately, children themselves are responsible for learning—and for applying the most useful understandings from demonstrations in sync with their own development.

Employment

Learners require time and opportunity to practice their evolving abilities with what is being learned. Children learning to talk, read, and write require time and opportunities to use their evolving language and skill development. As young learners seem to know intuitively, this practice or employment of language needs to occur both with others and when they are by themselves. Using their developing language and literacy skills allows children to practice and apply what they are learning about how language works; this helps them progress toward fluency.

Approximation

Learners approximate, or make attempts, when learning. As children learn to talk, they approximate when using language, and we respond to the meaning of their words. Responding to the intentions behind their messages honors their approximations as true and meaningful communication. The same must be true in all other learning experiences. There is no expectation for children to produce fully articulated responses and attempts before we respond to the meanings behind their approximations. We also don't expect that approximations, such as baby talk or invented spellings, will be permanent.

Response

When learning to talk, children receive responses, sometimes referred to as feedback from a more knowledgeable other, typically a parent, as they produce oral language. Similarly, they receive responses from a teacher as they read and write language. Communication between the learner and the significant other is honest and positive, with no hidden agenda. To be effective, responses occur in a timely and relevant fashion. And, importantly, the adult does not expect the child to immediately reproduce the exact response that was given by the adult, whether in that first moment or in future exchanges.

What Are the Processes That Empower Learning?

Cambourne's eight Conditions of Learning are complemented by four Processes That Empower Learning. The Processes describe the learner's exchanges and interactions with other learners and the content being learned. These exchanges support the durability and transferability of what is learned. In his ongoing research into classrooms where the Conditions are intentionally applied, teacher-to-student, student-to-teacher, and student-to-student discourse enables a series of learning processes to develop. These Processes are necessary to support the Conditions of Learning. They coexist seamlessly in classrooms and are difficult to separate. Again, this chapter presents a short definition of each process, and Chapter 8 elaborates more fully on each process. These are the four Processes identified so far in Brian's research:

Transformation

The Process of Transformation enables learners to construct the intended meanings from demonstrations with which they engage, in a manner that enables them to use and apply these meanings in other settings, events, and experiences. At the core of the Transformation process, enhanced through discussions, is deconstructing and reconstructing meanings about the concepts and knowledge involved in demonstrations. The approximations and decisions made by learners as they assume responsibility for their learning are inherent in these transformations. The opportunities teachers create for students to talk about their learning support transformation, leading to deeper meanings that transcend the immediate learning situation. Transformation isn't simply copying the person demonstrating or memorizing by rote what is being taught; learners actually transform what is learned into something that is uniquely theirs.

Discussion/Reflection

We learn best when we talk with others about our understandings. Talk with others (or, as is the case with reflection, talk with ourselves) about our thinking allows us to construct, clarify, interpret, adjust, and expand our understandings. The turn-and-talk times, the whole-class discussions, and the small-group work inherent in collaboration lead to understandings that can't be constructed independently. Discussion allows us to gauge our own thinking in relation to the thoughts of others—and to engage in a recursive applying–discussing–transforming–evaluating cycle of learning.

Application

Learners need opportunities to apply what they've engaged with, creating opportunities to approximate what they think they're supposed to be learning and get a response ("feedback") from a more knowledgeable "other." One form of Application is reflecting (talking to one's self) about what they've learned. While the definitions of Employment and Application are very similar, the subtle, but important, difference is in who determines what is being applied or employed. The Process of Application of what is being learned is enhanced by collaboration. Having students talk about their reading with partners during independent time is an example of collaboration. When people collaborate, application, discussion, and transformation occur, resulting in a multilayered experience that leads to greater understanding. Through this joint construction, and reflection on this joint construction, the new learning is further transformed.

Evaluation

While response from others is a Condition of Learning, self-evaluation of our own learning (what we learned) and learning process (how we learned) is also important. As we apply, discuss, and transform our learning, each of us evaluates our own performance by asking, "How am I doing?" Building reflection time into our teaching experiences supports this self-evaluation.

More to the Story
The Balanced Literacy Classroom

Classrooms applying the Conditions of Learning and the Processes That Empower Learning embody what we earlier referred to as a balanced pedagogy; they are also sometimes referred to as *balanced literacy classrooms*. These classrooms use instructional approaches such as read aloud and modeled writing, shared reading and writing, guided reading and writing, and independent reading and writing. A workshop approach may also be implemented to indicate and structure the relationships among these instructional practices. Phonics and word study are taught both implicitly and explicitly. The Processes That Empower Learning are central, underlying principles in these classrooms. Decisions made by teachers using these various instructional approaches can strengthen the Conditions and Processes by providing the physical, social, emotional, and intellectual spaces necessary for learning to occur.

Conclusion

Through the Conditions of Learning and the accompanying Processes, Brian offers a framework for considering the teaching decisions we make as we move toward a holistic instructional stance. We believe these Conditions and Processes can be universally applied to all instructional areas—literacy, math, science, social studies, and so on.

Each of the following chapters focuses on and expands the discussion of individual Conditions and Processes, presents classroom experiences, and then unpacks these classroom stories for how various teaching

Why we do things the way we do matters tremendously.

decisions made by the teacher affect the Conditions and, in turn, the learners. While each classroom story describes a single encounter, one can imagine the cumulative impact of ongoing instruction designed to strengthen the Conditions of Learning for children. Why we do things the way we do matters tremendously.

Thinking about Our Own Meaning-Making

- **Which of the Conditions of Learning resonate most with you at this time?**

- **How have these Conditions been present in learning you've experienced yourself?**

- **How have these Conditions been reflected in your own classroom practice?**

- **Which of these Processes That Empower Learning are you currently using in your own classroom? How do you feel they support your learners?**

- **What other big ideas are you holding as you reflect on this chapter? What questions do you have?**

"Thinking well together leads to thinking well alone."
——Peter H. Johnston, *Opening Minds: Using Language to Change Lives*

Chapter 4

Immersion and Demonstration

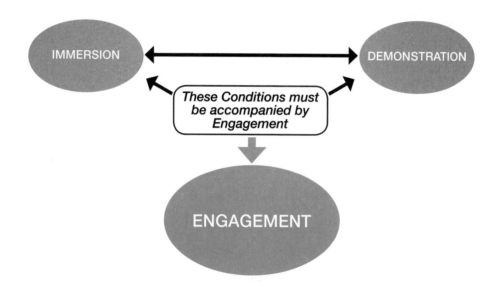

In the era of successful companies that have affected our day-to-day lives, no one can question that Apple Inc. has changed the lives of nearly everyone across the globe in some way, whether you actually use Apple's products or not. Simon Sinek, in *Start With Why: How Great Leaders Inspire Everyone to Take Action* (2009), cites Apple as an example of an organization that leads. He differentiates between leaders and those who lead. "Leaders hold a position of power or influence. Those who lead inspire us. . . . We follow those who lead not because we have to, but because we want to."

Apple cofounder and CEO Steve Jobs (1997) shared that the hardest part in effecting change is in understanding how what we are doing fits into a "cohesive, larger vision." This vision, Jobs said, starts with the "customer experience." What many people and companies do, instead, he went on to say, is to focus on the "what," creating a set of "little fixes" for each little problem that arises. A "cohesive, larger vision," Jobs concluded, considers what benefits we can give and where, ultimately, we can take customers. Customer experience, for Apple, is the company's focus, its "why"; technology, its "what," flows from that point.

Inspiring Literate Learners

How might this vision of "those who lead" apply to a classroom using the Conditions of Learning as a framework? No matter how many business analogies are offered, our children aren't "customers"—they don't choose us, nor we them. Even if we disagree or disappoint one another, most likely, we will be together for at least one school year—there is no cancellation policy. Neither are we, at day's end, trying to convince or persuade customers to make a purchase—what is to be learned isn't really negotiable. As leaders in our classrooms and schools, however, there are some relevant aspects to ponder in this analogy. To paraphrase Sinek's subtitle, isn't it the job of every teacher, as someone who leads in schools and classrooms, to "inspire everyone to take action"?

In a classroom, our "larger, cohesive vision"—what we'll rename the *learner experience*—considers what benefits we can give students and where we can take them. The benefits and where we take learners include supporting our students to develop their own understandings of the roles literacy, numeracy, science, and history play in one's life. How we illuminate those roles implies teaching in ways that are authentic, meaningful, and relevant. These foundational beliefs are essential for the Conditions of Learning to thrive. And, to design and nurture this learner experience requires a teacher to have a deep knowledge of how literacy develops.

For example, a critical understanding our learners must develop about reading is how a reader purposefully constructs, deconstructs, and reconstructs meanings from the symbols (print and graphics) on a page. This reading process is active. Effective readers use and integrate sources of information (semantic, syntactic, and graphophonic). They decipher the letters, words, and visuals on the page. They anticipate what the text says and monitor for meanings being constructed. Readers notice any incongruence and mismatches between the text and their own thinking and self-correct along the way. And all this occurs as they expand ideas across multiple texts and authors. Through engaging in this active reading process, readers assume a responsibility for composing not only what a single text says but also the most comprehensive and relevant possible meanings from what multiple authors have written. Automaticity and flexibility with these reading behaviors, understandings, and attitudes are the hallmarks of effective reading. These are the kinds of reading skills that are "forever developing" (Johnston, 1997) and don't lend

More to the Story
Sources of Information in Reading

The sources of information we use to understand texts are grouped into three overlapping classifications known as semantic, syntactic, and graphophonic systems (Fountas and Pinnell, 2016; Clay, 1985; Goodman, 1965). The *semantic* or *meaning system* includes our background knowledge of content and ideas, and what we know about how texts work; vocabulary we can access; and our ability to access information provided through illustrations and graphics. The evolving meanings we are making as we progress through the entire text are also considered semantic sources of information (Weaver, 1994). The *syntactic system*, or structure sources, includes grammatical knowledge such as word order and function words (like *as*, *of*, and *for*). Natural language and academic language patterns and structures are also part of the syntactic system. The *graphophonic system*, or visual sources of information, includes our understandings about individual letters and sounds as well as patterns of letters and sounds. Print conventions such as understanding the concepts of a word, a space between words, and punctuation are also an important part of this written language system.

Effective readers rarely show attention to an individual source of information but search and anticipate, check and confirm, and monitor and self-correct using all three systems simultaneously (Fountas and Pinnell, 2016; Weaver, 1994; Clay, 1985; Goodman, 1965). The efficient integration of these information systems is a hallmark of proficient readers, those who read for understanding ideas and meanings and do so within the privacy of their own heads as they read silently. Emergent and early readers, on the other hand, tend to rely more heavily on any one of the systems, thus requiring teachers to demonstrate using all three systems in an integrated fashion to read a text and comprehend the meanings intended by the author. Proficient readers use these meanings from this individual text as they construct, deconstruct, and reconstruct their ever-changing knowledge, understandings, feelings, values, and skills about literacy, literacy learning, and literacy use.

themselves to the concept of "mastery." Reading is meaning-making.

This active reading process allows for the multitude of pleasures reading brings. Readers may learn something they didn't know before, broadening their thinking or curiosity about a topic. As Vicki Vinton (2011) wrote, "We need to let them see how books can inform lives, giving us a wider, expanded vision of who we are, who we might become, and how we might engage with the world." Readers may vicariously experience something never before envisioned, expanding the possibilities and options in their lifetime of choices. Readers may be moved to cry or laugh as they empathize with a protagonist, perhaps informing personal decisions to be made in the future. Readers may, in fact, experience all these things simultaneously. "Reading has as many functions as the human body, and . . . not all of them are cerebral" (Quindlen, 1998).

Often, however, this full and rich view of reading isn't one that students seem to fashion for themselves. Recently, when Debra asked the question, "How do you know if you're understanding the book you're reading?" of a group of second graders she was teaching, a student replied, "You can say all the words on the page." When Debra probed by asking, "How else do you know?" the second response was, "You know the words on the page." When asked "How else do you know if you're understanding what you're reading?" there was a quiet period during which students looked at one other, looked at the ground, looked at the ceiling . . . but had nothing else to offer. Now, these were readers who live readerly lives through daily reading and writing workshops. Their teacher had demonstrated repeatedly that reading is about meaning-making. Somehow, the students weren't understanding what it means to be "participatory, self-directed, and multidimensional" as they process a text (Luke and Freebody, 1990). We asked ourselves how readers in

---

More to the Story

Understanding Literacy through Luke and Freebody's Four Resources Model of Reading

A framework for understanding and describing literacy can be helpful as we work to support our young learners. One such framework proposed by researchers Allan Luke and Peter Freebody (1990) identifies four roles, or resources, which readers and writers employ as they make sense of a text. Each of these resources is detailed below. A fuller explanation of this model of reading can be found in The Four Resources Model for Reading and Viewing (Victoria State Government, 2018).

Text Decoder	Text Participant
As readers break the code of language, they recognize and use alphabetic knowledge, sounds in words, spelling, punctuation, and patterns of sentence structure and text. Text decoders understand the relationship between spoken and written language. They can interpret graphic symbols and their contexts of use. They understand and apply knowledge of the "technology" of written language (Hornsby, 2000).	As readers participate in the meaning of text, they understand and compose meaningful written, visual, and spoken texts considering the cultures in which the text was constructed. Text participants understand the meaning patterns operating in written texts. These readers make literal and inferential meanings of texts. They draw on and apply knowledge of the topic, text structure, and syntax to make sense of a text (Hornsby, 2000).
Text User	**Text Analyst**
As readers use texts functionally, they understand how texts are used to perform various functions in society, both inside and outside of school. They understand how the function of texts and use of various text types impact a text's structure, tone, and components.	As readers critically analyze and transform texts, they understand how texts are constructed to represent (or silence) particular points of view. These readers understand that texts are not neutral but are crafted to reflect the values, views, and interests of an author, through both words and graphics.

classrooms where they are immersed in daily reading experiences continue to believe understanding is about saying the words correctly. And what might knowing this about our learners and about literacy mean for future demonstrations?

Inspiring Action through Our Leadership

Even though teachers strive to create learner experiences that inspire students, despite our best efforts, many children in classrooms today believe reading to be first and foremost about decoding the symbols on the page. This can be true even in classrooms where teachers demonstrate otherwise. (Remember, you are not your students' only teacher.) Many literacy demonstrations that students experience—whether conducted by parents, other teachers, or even other children—may overemphasize the letters and sounds, words and sentences. The immersive experiences and the demonstrations of literacy for many students highlight the component parts of written text in isolation. Demonstrations may also be unclear or, possibly, inaccurate in their delivery. Whatever the case, the vision of reading, for some students, becomes skewed; the learners develop "reading knots" (Clay, 1982). Clay hypothesized that such children "had tangled the teaching in a web of distorted learning which blocked school progress."

While the component parts are important (one struggles to make meaning independently without them), the reasons we read or write aren't to know letters and sounds and words. An active reading process requires not only understanding the letters, sounds, words, and sentences individually but also orchestrating these smaller pieces into coherent wholes. The parts, as they are studied, are in service of greater understandings. Many demonstrations don't necessarily help students understand how the parts contribute to the ultimate learner experience of making meaning. And, even when students do have strong cognitive experiences in lessons supported by thoughtful teachers, sometimes, our demonstrations don't extend to showing students exactly how we got to the meanings we made.

As teachers in constructivist classrooms, we must present lessons that embody the construct–deconstruct–reconstruct journey to meaning. Immersion and Demonstration must illustrate *all* the practices outlined in the Four Resources Model (Luke and Freebody, 1999) in order for learners to envision a complete, dynamic, and orchestrated reading experience. Lessons with texts begin with readers constructing initial understandings; these lessons, however, involve much more than "gist." Deepening understandings take time and multiple opportunities for readers to consider and reconsider their own understandings, thinking alongside others while in their company. The role of the teacher is that of facilitator, not the giver of ideas. The purpose of these kinds of lessons is to support learners as they begin to understand literacy as a collection of practices that are "dynamic, being redeveloped, recombined, and articulated in relation to one another on an ongoing basis" (Luke and Freebody, 1999). In other words, literate people move among these practices as they make meaning of a text, not in a prescribed order as is sometimes presented to students in some misguided formula for reading closely.

How a teacher becomes "someone who leads" is explored in the rest of this chapter. We begin with a discussion of Immersion and Demonstration. These two Conditions contribute to lessons that are designed to be meaning-based, purpose-driven, and both strategy- and skill-applied. Next, we visit a classroom that showcases these two powerful Conditions being nurtured. We unpack the classroom experiences to highlight teaching decisions that brought Immersion and Demonstration to life.

Thinking about Our Own Meaning-Making

- **How do you define reading?**

- **How might your definition influence the messages about reading that you communicate to your learners?**

Immersion as a Condition of Learning

Immersion provides opportunities to surround students with what it is they are learning, so they experience the intellectual, physical, and emotional aspects of the something being learned. Immersion allows for the full, rich learner experience, an opportunity to be saturated in or by what is being learned. If these immersions are significant—in other words, if engagement is occurring—for the students, they attend to what is happening during the immersions and demonstrations. Otherwise, the intended learning from the immersion or demonstration simply washes over them, without leaving much residue.

When learning a language, children are surrounded by whole, meaningful examples of the language; in a sense, they are saturated by language (Cambourne, 1988). While the specific language may be different across cultures, children learn their native language within this cultural context. As they interact with more-knowledgeable others, they see the effects of language use, both in the language others use and in their own use. They hear and attempt not only words but also the sounds, rhythms, and cadences of the language they are learning. In this back-and-forth among language users, the meanings provided by these models are built through the context in which the language is produced. Because this language is contextualized, it makes sense.

Immersion in this same participatory, contextualized fashion in what they are learning about literacy matters tremendously to young students. With respect to literacy, in a classroom built on constructivist principles, children regularly experience examples of reading and writing in the context of meaning-making. They see and hear texts read aloud to them and written with them each day, and these sessions offer them multiple opportunities to think and talk with others about meanings they are making. Vocabulary and language structures expand with each and every opportunity to engage in hearing language, interacting with language, and producing language to co-construct meanings with their classmates and teachers.

Learners produce and see writing (their own and that of others), and they share reading and writing daily to communicate messages about their lives and the lives of others. This saturation of written language, provided and guided by the observant teacher, reinforces the knowledge and skills to be learned over time and establishes an understanding of the purposes of written language. Within these immersive experiences, students learn the purpose of those squiggly things we call letters, sounds, and words, connecting them to a desire to communicate meaning. These kinds of learning experiences build on the language children bring to school and help them view their home language as a positive and culturally sensitive basis for making meaning.

While some people may equate this way of thinking about Immersion as merely a form of "incidental learning," *incidental* is a poor word choice because it trivializes the process. When one is put intentionally into a position of witnessing something to be learned, what may appear to be incidental takes on considerably more relevance. The immersion becomes more purposeful to the learner.

Thinking about Our Own Meaning-Making

• **What immersive experiences do you provide for your students on a regular basis?**

Demonstration as a Condition of Learning

As we stated earlier in Chapter 3, all learning begins when one engages with a demonstration of some kind. In a classroom, demonstrations give us opportunities to unpack immersive experiences with learners so they might more closely examine and refine what they learned within that experience for themselves. Explicit demonstrations of how readers and writers make meanings create the basis of modeling. Demonstrations must occur multiple times, and in multiple modes, because learners engage with different features or characteristics of our demonstrations, regardless of our explicit lesson focus.

Demonstrations must occur multiple times, and in multiple modes, because learners engage with different features or characteristics of our demonstrations, regardless of our explicit lesson focus.

When learning to talk, learners experience clear demonstrations of language use. Verbal demonstrations are often combined with a physical demonstration of what language can accomplish. For example, a request to "pass the salt" is accompanied by someone actually passing the saltshaker to the person who requests it. This verbal and physical demonstration provided by a parent or some other participant illustrates the function or purpose of the language (i.e., to inquire or request). It also illustrates an action to accompany the language (e.g., passing the salt) and an example of a language structure (i.e., the wording or expression adjusted for complexity based on the sophistication of the learner). This "thinking aloud" about the message in the mind of the person speaking, along with a physical demonstration, provides an effective model of how language works.

Demonstrations may include artifacts (books or other written content) and/or actions (physical acts that show the effects of language). Without language-rich, interactive demonstrations, language learning is not likely to occur. This is why simply putting children in front of a television or just surrounding them with books isn't enough to ensure that learning occurs.

The most effective demonstrations begin with language "wholes," meaning the demonstration is complete and rich enough to be meaningful. Beginning with a language "whole" allows a learner to see and understand the processes necessary for creating an approximation of this demonstration in other settings.

It's difficult to be metacognitive when you haven't been cognitive in the first place!

In some ways, starting with a "whole" experience may seem counterintuitive. "Common-sense" approaches to learning often begin with learning the bits and putting those bits together, and someday a learner gets to a "whole." David N. Perkins, in *Making Learning Whole: How Seven Principles of Teaching Can Transform Education* (2009), refers to this as *elementitis*, in which we focus on the elements rather than the whole. Even in lessons focusing on parts or skills or a strategy, that part or skill or strategy must connect back to meaning, which is available only if the reader has made that meaning to begin with. It's difficult to be metacognitive when you haven't been cognitive in the first place!

As a teacher explains a part/skill/strategy, he or she must include a response to this question: "How does knowing about this part/skill/strategy help us get to the meaning?" This is the difference between teaching our students to know or name a part or skill or strategy as item knowledge and teaching our students to be strategic. In this way, we support our learners to continually revisit how parts/skills/strategies help us get to bigger meanings.

Mismatch between Theory and Practice
"Doing" versus "Using"

As teachers conclude literacy-skill lessons, they may say things like:

- "As you're reading today, see if you can find the new word we are learning. This will help you be a good reader."
- "Today in writing, be sure to use capitals and periods. And always write in complete sentences."
- "Fill in your graphic organizer before you start writing. This will make your writing better."

While these are all skills or tools literate people may use, each is only used in certain situations at certain times for certain purposes. In other words, their use is always conditional.

Consider a graphic organizer, a helpful tool for highlighting structure and big concepts. Sometimes writers choose to use a graphic organizer; sometimes, though, they don't. Sometimes they use them early in a project, sometimes later. Sometimes they rework the graphic organizer along the way; sometimes they abandon it completely for a different organizer as their thinking changes. In any case, the use of a graphic organizer is conditional as determined by the writer.

In a demonstration of any skill or tool, ensure learners understand not only the declarative, or item, knowledge (what the skill is) but also the procedural and conditional knowledge—how, when, where, and why a learner uses the skill or tool. This approach presents a complete demonstration of the skill or tool in context. It supports intentional decision-making by a learner and makes what is demonstrated more likely to be applied by the learner in the future.

Thinking about Our Own Meaning-Making

- **What holistic demonstrations do you provide for your students on a regular basis?**

Into the Classroom for Read Alouds

It was early spring in Trish Candia's kindergarten class, and all the students were gathered on the rug, preparing to hear, think, and talk about a new story. The energy was palpable; joy revealed itself through bright eyes, big smiles, and wiggling bodies as the children settled in to engage with this text. While the home

---

More to the Story
Why Read Aloud Matters So Very Much

In Steven Layne's *"In Defense of Read Aloud: Sustaining Best Practice"* (2015), Brian refers to read aloud as "the Swiss Army Knife" of instructional practices. Widely used by teachers, this powerful literacy approach encourages contextualized skill or strategy instruction, as described in the Conditions of Immersion and Demonstration. Often thought of as an approach used only by teachers of young children, read aloud is compelling and effective support for children in all grades engaging in the meaning-making process.

In the first reading of a text, a community of readers commences the journey of constructing meaning. Through multiple rereads, those same readers construct, deconstruct, and reconstruct meanings, considering multiple perspectives as they talk with peers about the text being shared by their thoughtful teacher. Through read aloud experiences, a community of "we" emerges, one where text ideas and language often serve as shorthand for shared meanings. Read aloud has an amazing ability to change and improve any horrible, no-good, very bad day, taming any wild things with the magic trick of children's literature.

---

language of many of the students in the classroom was a language other than English, reading, thinking, and talking together had started on day one of school for these children, and they clearly understood how this read aloud experience worked!

The text was a powerful picture book, *The Other Side* written by Jacqueline Woodson and illustrated by Earl B. Lewis (2001). In this story, Clover and Annie are two young girls who are told they can't be friends. "Clover's mom says it isn't safe to cross the fence that segregates their African-American side of town from the white side where Annie lives. But the two girls strike up a friendship and get around the grown-ups' rules by sitting on top of the fence together."

This text choice that morning was a bit unusual in that it wasn't made strictly by the teacher herself; the entire school chose to read a common text to build school-wide community. Earlier that week, as Trish and her coach, Debra, worked together to plan a lesson series using the text, they wondered about the meanings and understandings these kindergartners might make with a book typically used with older students. While there might be layers of meaning the young students wouldn't understand because of their ages, Trish and Debra agreed that there were several ideas they expected the students to discuss: the challenges inherent in making new friends, the feelings that surface when you're told you can't be friends with someone, and how people and friendships change during the course of a story.

Their current literacy unit had been going on for a few weeks, with two key ideas driving the text selections and focuses for the lessons: 1) understanding how the physical and emotional aspects of characters in the story are revealed to readers and 2) noticing how and why characters often change in some way throughout a story. Alongside this work, the students were learning ways of thinking and talking about books to strengthen their discussions with partners and in groups.

In addition to the work in the current unit, earlier in the school year, the children had determined (and charted) things literate people think and talk about: their favorite parts of a text (and their "not-favorite" parts, in kindergarten lingo!), connections between a book and their lives or other books, patterns throughout a text, and wonderings they had about the text (Chambers, 1993). And, if the other person (or persons) didn't know the book being discussed, sharing a little about it could help foster understanding.

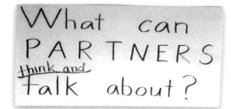

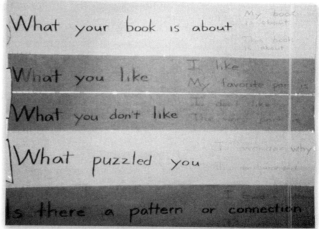

Keeping in mind the prior thinking and discussing of texts that had occurred and the current literacy and talk goals, Trish and Debra crafted a lesson for a first reading of the text. They intended the students to get to know the story in this first reading. They also planned to meet again after the first reading to consider possible revisits to the text.

The First Reading

During the first reading of *The Other Side*, the students were quite engaged by Woodson's touching story of Clover and Annie and their budding friendship. As Trish slowly read the text aloud, she paused periodically for the children to share their thinking with their partners and the group. The students quickly recognized Clover's and Annie's curiosity about each other and their desire to be friends. They easily predicted that the two girls would figure out a way to be friends, because that's how stories and life often happen. They related relevant personal connections that involved being told they couldn't play with others and the feelings that arose as a result.

While the metaphorical and historical meanings layered in the text were beyond comprehension for kindergartners, Trish felt they had constructed some solid understandings as a first layer of meaning from this initial read. She also believed they were capable of understanding more deeply.

Revisiting the Text to Deepen Meaning

As Trish and the students revisited the text on the following day, the students continued to notice connections, and, in this rereading of the entire text, Trish listened for opportunities to help the students understand why their connections mattered, to bring a metacognitive awareness to their reading experience. Ashley, a student in the class, recalled how someone in her preschool wouldn't let her play on the swings.

Ashley: *She said I couldn't swing 'cause I wasn't big enough and I said yes, I was, but she still wouldn't let me play.*

Trish: *How did you feel when the girl wouldn't let you play?*

Ashley: *I felt sad. I almost cried but I didn't.*

Trish: *So, Ashley, you felt sad when someone said you couldn't play. How do you think Annie feels when Sandra (another character in the story) says no, Annie can't jump rope with us?*

Ashley: *She feels sad.*

Trish: (to the class) *When Ashley remembered how sad she felt when someone wouldn't let her play, Ashley knew how Annie felt when Sandra told Annie she couldn't play.*

Trish referred back to the book, showing several relevant illustrations to the students, including ones where the character, Sandra, told Annie she couldn't play with her, Clover, and the other friends.

Trish: *Connections can help us understand how characters are feeling in a story. They make the story more interesting to us and make us want to know more about our characters. Thank you, Ashley, for helping us understand how our connections help us understand the stories we read.*

Trish read on in the story. A few pages later, she read this section from the book, where the illustration shows Clover's mother hanging laundry while Clover plays nearby:

> *"Some mornings my mama watched us. I waited for her to tell me to get down from that fence before I break my neck or something. But she never did.*
>
> *"'I see you made a new friend,' she said one morning."*

Trish paused, and silence hung in the air. After a few seconds of quiet, Maya spoke up.

Maya: *I wonder why her mama changed her mind.*

Trish was silent, allowing time and space for other students to respond to Maya's "wondering." No one did. Trish hesitated, as if she wanted to say something, then continued reading to the end of the story.

When Trish and Debra met to debrief the first reading and plan the next day's lesson, Trish noted Maya's brilliant wondering near the end of the lesson. Then she shared every teacher's big fear: "I didn't know what to do!" Debra assured her that not knowing what to do is a common experience for all teachers and that, sometimes, it's better not to do something if you're unsure of what to do.

As it turned out, Trish had done the most important teacher thinking herself: recognizing that Maya's wondering was important. At that point, Debra just nudged her, asking, "Now that you've had some time to think, what do you wish you'd done in that moment?" Trish's response became the focus for the following day's lesson.

Revisiting the Text Again to Go Farther

The next day Trish's lesson used only a two-page illustrated spread in *The Other Side*, the pages that had prompted Maya's wondering. As Trish believes a wondering contains an implicit question, she decided to reframe the wondering as a question.

Trish: *Today we are going to think and talk about only one place in the story.*

(Trish showed the illustration and reread the page before continuing with the discussion.)

> *Yesterday, when we read this page, Maya asked an important question. She asked: Why did Clover's mama change her mind? We didn't talk about Maya's question. Last night, I kept thinking about Maya's question, and I wondered what ideas you have about her question.*

(Trish indicated a chart where she had written Maya's question.)

Maya, can you share your question again?

Maya: (reading the chart to support herself) *Why did Clover's mama change her mind?*

Trish: (to the class): *Why do you think Clover's mama changed her mind? Turn to your partners.*

Students turned to partners and discussed Maya's question. Then several partnerships shared thinking with the whole group (e.g., "Her mama wanted her to have a friend." "Clover wanted to be friends and her mama let her." "Her mama thinks Annie is a nice friend."). After the discussion, Trish shared her reflections on the thinking that had just occurred.

Trish: *As readers, we have been thinking about why characters change in stories. Maya noticed a change in Clover's mama's thinking. She wondered why Clover's mama had changed her thinking about Clover and Annie's friendship. Maya's question helped us think more about why a character in the story changed. Thinking about characters—how they think and feel and how they change in stories—helps us understand stories even more.*

This lesson offered every student the opportunity to think and talk with others about why characters change in stories. The discussion also gave Trish more opportunities to notice and name the effective reading and thinking work students were doing as readers. In the next section, we unpack the teaching decisions Trish made that strengthened the Immersion and Demonstration her students encountered.

Teaching Decisions Affecting Immersion and Demonstration

Teaching is designing opportunities to increase the potential for meaning-making for learners. Teachers play a major role in developing the spaces in which these opportunities for making meaning occur. To make learning as fail-safe and barrier-free as possible, teachers anticipate what students need in order to learn. Teachers intentionally design environments to eliminate complications and obstacles to learning to maximize the probability of success, which results in durable understandings. This, however, doesn't mean working to eliminate every problem that might arise

Teaching is designing opportunities to increase the potential for meaning-making for learners.

or discouraging approximations. Learning to be a problem finder and problem solver requires encountering problems to find and solve. Teachers in constructivist classrooms view challenges as opportunities for learning. An environment, or ecology, that provides opportunities for learning includes a focus on the physical, social, emotional, and intellectual settings for learning.

As we unpack the classroom lesson, we will explore four categories of instructional decisions (Space and Time, Routines and Behaviors, Materials and Resources, and Teacher Thinking and Language). We will also highlight their effects on the Conditions of Immersion and Demonstration.

Space and Time

In Trish's classroom, her belief in the power of immersing learners (many of whom speak a language other than English at home) in language, thinking, and talking is reflected in the daily schedules and the physical environment of the classroom. Gathering students to think and talk together about texts occurs

---

More to the Story
Physical/Social Spaces

The physical ecology of the classroom is usually determined by the teacher. The decisions a teacher makes about physical space can encourage social interaction among the learners, or hinder it. In her book, *In the Company of Children* (1996), Joanne Hindley quotes her colleague Isabel Beaton saying:

> "I can put up barriers to communication or I can set things up to encourage conversation. I can establish lonely islands of I's or I can form communities and provinces of we's. Everyone can have his or her own of each thing or groups can share. I can make that sharing difficult or I can support it. All the energy in the room can come from me or I can have constellations of energy. And the geography I put in place will do that for me (page 5)."

Classrooms are ecological settings and are subject to the same principles that determine and explain how other settings work the way they do. They are a mix of inanimate objects—such as furniture, wall charts, shelves, books, and tools for reading and writing—and the people, or inhabitants, who enter the setting, all with different roles, responsibilities, and authority. The inhabitants in classrooms behave in highly predictable ways. Certain routines and behaviors are so ingrained, they are known to even the youngest inhabitants and are even parodied (for example, raising hands to speak or waving a hand to attract attention from the teacher).

Changing the physical ecology of a classroom is more than just changing the furniture and tools; the change can craft a completely different way of being together for teachers and for students.

multiple times throughout the day, in read aloud sessions, shared reading, and shared and interactive writing. Each of these instructional approaches offers multiple opportunities to demonstrate literacy skills and strategies in the context of constructing or deconstructing meaningful texts.

Trish plans for lengthier sessions of read aloud on some days. These demonstrations honor the notion that thinking and talking well takes time. She has space in which students can gather in various configurations, including a circle; adapting the space as desired acknowledges that room arrangements can either support or hinder students' abilities to think and talk together.

Thinking about Our Own Meaning-Making

• How do you organize classroom space and time to support student meaning-making?

Routines and Behaviors

Trish regularly plans revisits to familiar texts, knowing that each rereading offers her another opportunity to demonstrate more about literacy. The students have multiple opportunities to notice something else within each text that might have escaped their attention in other readings. These same texts are also made available for students to revisit independently and with partners to continue their thinking and learning.

Turning and talking about your thinking is taught right from the beginning in Trish's classroom and is intentionally planned for in her lessons. Students recognize that their role in discussion is to share ideas with and receive ideas from other learners. They're well on their way to "developing processes that enable them to navigate their environment, and each other, with care, respect, and trust" (Nichols, 2019a). This interactive nature of learning strengthens the immersive and demonstrative experiences of literacy for the learners. Attending to social and emotional aspects of our classroom ecology through the language we use positions learners as capable and agentive beings (Johnston, 2012). Social/emotional learning can't be an add-on to our teaching or something we "do" in morning meetings. It's far too essential to learning and permeates every learning situation.

More to the Story
Social/Emotional Space

A prime example of social and emotional aspects arising within the interactions with students occurs at the beginning of lessons when a teacher asks a question to determine what knowledge children have on a specific topic. If we ask, "Have you ever been to the zoo?" the student must rely on direct experience. Many children will be unable to respond beyond a simple no, and the student is now positioned as someone with a deficit, someone without knowledge.

By changing the question to "What do you know about zoos?" we position the learners differently. We position them as knowledgeable people who can, in effect, help us understand what they know about the topic of zoos (which is what we really wanted to know anyway). Follow-up questions such as "Where did you learn that?" or "How did you find out about that?" can help us learn more about the students' lives and experiences. Our questions help us focus on what students do have (vicarious knowledge gained from television, movies, books, and other children) rather than what they may or may not have (direct experience).

This kind of teacher thinking is exemplified through the language of meaning-making. Comprehension, in these classrooms, isn't viewed as a thing we have or don't have; comprehending is the process of meaning-making. These deliberate interactions occur throughout the school day and offer us concrete ways to demonstrate our belief in children's abilities. These kinds of interactions also offer us opportunities to recognize the potential in all learners.

Thinking about Our Own Meaning-Making

• **What routines and behaviors do you use to support your learners?**

• **How do they support meaning-making?**

Materials and Resources

Trish chooses a variety of books to use during the days and weeks of instruction. She holds dear the concept of quality children's literature—stories that generate empathy and understanding of others, and informational texts that inspire and satisfy the curiosity of her learners. She brings Gay Ivey's (2010) statement to life: "Instead of focusing on how to get students to remember what they read, our best bet is to provide texts that are more memorable."

Trish also has intimate knowledge of quality leveled texts to support her readers, texts that are constructed with big ideas worth talking about and opportunities for learners to apply and develop their knowledge of how letters, sounds, and words work. These books will enable them to read more-complex texts for themselves one day. The purposes of each kind of text play a role throughout Trish's instructional environment, contributing to the students' immersion in texts and increasing her opportunities for demonstrations.

> ## Thinking about Our Own Meaning-Making
>
> • **What materials and resources do you use to support your learners?**
>
> • **How do you use them to support meaning-making?**

Teacher Thinking and Language

In the first reading of a book, Trish constructs a lesson with pauses for discussion, using broad questions such as "What are you thinking?" rather than directing students toward particular ideas through heavily directive questions. This broad question approach helps Trish understand exactly what meanings the students are constructing and what, in the text, they may have overlooked; these reflections, in turn, provide keen insight into what is important for her next demonstrations. She probes student responses with statements like "Say more about that" or questions like "What makes you think that?" to elicit more language and thinking about their ideas.

More to the Story
Using Broad Prompts to Support Student Thinking

The questions and prompts on this chart are broad in nature, to invite students to share what they think rather than take ideas from a question and turn it into an "answer."

Key Prompts for Engaging Thinkers	
Teacher Prompt	**Intention in Using**
Silence.	Giving students time to think
What are you thinking?	Inviting students to explain what they think
Tell us more.	Inviting students to expand on their thinking
What makes you think that?	Inviting students to share the context that led to thinking
What in the text got you thinking that?	Inviting students to share details from the text that led to thinking
What do you think about _____'s idea?	Inviting students to consider another's perspective

Often, the revisits to texts in Trish's classroom are driven by her students' thinking. Trish listens carefully to their comments, seeking opportunities to help them become metacognitive about the thinking they are doing. Her work values what they say and feel. Furthermore, she recognizes the importance of those two key elements for learning, so the students become confident and able thinkers in other settings. The most effective teachers notice what students are attending to, what the learners *are* doing, rather than focusing primarily on deficits or gaps. They highlight student effort and support children to notice their own attempts and processes. In this way, we increase the learner's awareness of their "foothold in print" (Clay, 1998).

While the classroom exchange detailed previously focused on Trish's work with kindergartners, this same kind of learning and teaching is equally apparent when she teaches intermediate-grade students. From the first day of instruction, Trish keeps the focus squarely on meaning, and any strategy or skill work is in service of that meaning. She takes students' ideas seriously and responds to meanings the students are making. And, when misunderstandings about a text arise, Trish assumes an assessment stance: Approximations and miscues are windows into how learners process, what they've attended to in the text, and what they have missed or ignored.

Deeper meanings don't necessarily come from reading more-complex texts but instead from opportunities to think about a text in more-complex ways.

Trish understands that deeper meanings don't necessarily come from reading more-complex texts but instead come from opportunities to think about a text in more-complex ways (Nichols, 2019a, 2019b; Vinton, 2017). Therefore, the learners in her classrooms take their work seriously and expect to be thinkers. Rereading is viewed as one way to learn more; talking

---

More to the Story
Intellectual Spaces

Children grow into the intellectual spaces that surround them, to paraphrase Vygotsky. In sync with a constructivist stance, a teacher deliberately orchestrates the classroom ecology in ways to subtly ensure that students engage in authentic learning experiences; those experiences, in turn, are reinforced by extended student-centered discussions of the meanings they are constructing. Young students learn language through how it is used to communicate meaning being made. Teachers constantly observe what children are doing or saying, or attempting to do or say, rather than focusing on their deficits; their goal is to gauge the depth of understandings being developed. Teachers and children view tentative understandings that develop more fully over time as processes both "of" and "for" learning. Learning, in these spaces, is seen as a flexible and ever-changing journey.

with partners and other learners is another. As the students work with partners during whole-group time and, later, during independent times with those same partners, they are immersed in discussions about reading and writing that build not only language and vocabulary but also the mindful habits for thinking well.

Conclusion

Teachers routinely make decisions during the course of school days and school years. The Conditions of Learning underpin each and every one of those teaching and learning decisions. The quality of those decisions, or lack thereof, is determined by how those decisions either support or hinder learning. To gauge instruction in any other terms places greater value on what the teacher is doing than on what is actually happening for the learner.

Brian's research indicates that teachers who understand the Conditions of Learning at a deep level view teaching as the creation of opportunities to apply the Conditions and Processes. This definition of teaching underpins a framework for intentional teaching decisions. These teachers *deliberately* nurture the Conditions and Processes, linking intentional Immersion and Demonstration to topics, ideas, concepts, skills, and strategies. There is nothing incidental nor accidental about the choices teachers make as they expose students to high-quality literacy materials and authentic literacy experiences and craft explicit instruction based on student needs. These intentional teaching decisions affect the Conditions and the Processes significantly.

More to the Story
Going Deeper with Our Teaching Examples

Each instructional transcript included in this book was deliberately chosen for the chapter in which it appears. The challenge in discussing these Conditions individually is the considerable tttamong all the Conditions. Because all the Conditions and Processes are interrelated and synergistic, each is present in different degrees in every instructional moment. In Chapter 9, we discuss Trish's lesson in relation to all the Conditions and Processes. Our thinking about the Conditions and Processes for additional lessons in other chapters is detailed in Chapter 9.

In the final lesson linking to *The Other Side*, Trish began not with a question she had but with Maya's question. Rather than creating a lesson to model her thinking or coming up with text-dependent questions or thinking about activities connected to the text, she immersed the students in a discussion of a classmate's question. Using students' questions or comments to help guide discussion and to help us understand what needs more attention ultimately provides us with finely tuned

Using students' questions or comments to help guide discussion and to help us understand what needs more attention ultimately provides us with finely tuned opportunities for demonstrations based on what students need in order to learn. In this way, Immersion and Demonstration deepen Engagement as students develop a vision of themselves as learners and understand why what is happening in the classroom is important for their lives. This exchange gives them something to work toward. In our next chapter, we explore the Condition of Engagement and how to further support students as they develop a vision for themselves as learners.

Thinking about Our Own Meaning-Making

- How do you describe the reading and writing process for yourself?

- How do these beliefs affect the Conditions of Immersion and Demonstration for your students?

- Consider the Immersion and Demonstration you have provided for your students. What mismatches exist between your theory of learning and the Immersion and Demonstration you provide?

- How do you intentionally construct your Immersion and Demonstration to be "someone who leads?

- What other big ideas are you holding as you reflect on this chapter? What questions do you have?

"Have you noticed no one ever says 'mind and heart'?
That's because if we win a person's heart, the engagement, effort, and intellect of
the mind are more likely to follow."

———Regie Routman, *Literacy Essentials: Engagement, Excellence, and Equity for All Learners*

Chapter 5

Engagement

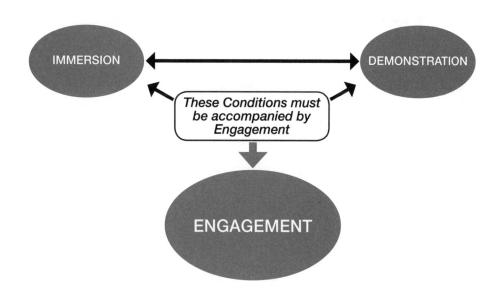

"I wonder why her mama changed her mind." (Maya, age five)

*"Do you hear it, Ms. Candia? There's **and** in Jack and Jill'!"* (Cameron, age six)

"Don't tell us! Let us figure it out!" (Jorge, age eight)

For these learners, their engagement is visceral and cerebral, social and individual. All the young learners who shared these powerful observations about their own thinking would be deemed *engaged*. We all recognize engagement when we see it. Readers lose themselves in books, "losing" their present—their time, location, and being—to the one revealed within the book. Writers stare upward, pursuing words to voice their ideas, seeking to convey their meanings to others. As teachers, we acknowledge this pursuit and effort as signs of true engagement.

And then, our teacher thoughts move to reflecting and wondering how to support this kind of engagement to occur more frequently, more reliably, and more pervasively. We know its importance; we want to know its genesis. We want to fuel it and foster it. We want to amplify it and articulate it. How we do that is the basis of this chapter.

What Do We Mean by Engagement?

Engagement is fundamental to learning. It's complex and difficult to define because it incorporates a range of behaviors on the part of the learner. It has overtones of "attention" and "attending" associated with it. While reading teachers have specific meanings for the words *attention* and *attending*, here we use the commonplace definition for both. Learning is unlikely to occur if the potential learner doesn't *attend* to, or notice, what is being demonstrated. The potential learner is unlikely to attend if she or he doesn't perceive a need or purpose for the learning.

Learning anything involves a desire—a desire to be able to do, or know about, what is being observed, whether it is happening in real time and space, in one's imagination, or by means of the virtual realities of our digital devices. Connotations

---

More to the Story
How I Perceive the Difference between Interest, Motivation, and Engagement by Brian Cambourne

I love to watch the hang gliders soaring above the cliffs near my university. The grace and freedom they're obviously experiencing and the sheer adventure of what they're doing force me to observe them whenever they're around. They fascinate me, and I find the spectacle extremely compelling. I observe these demonstrations with an awestruck incredulity. *Although I'm a fascinated observer of these demonstrations, I do not engage with them.* If someone asked me to draw an accurate representation of a hang glider, or to describe the materials from which one is made—or to describe the uses of the appendages and straps and harnesses that are an integral part of one—I would be hard put to do so. I have observed. I am fascinated, interested, and highly motivated to watch, but I have not engaged, and no learning of any significance has occurred. Why not?

Simply because I do not see myself as a potential hang glider. Furthermore, I truly cannot see how taking up hang gliding at my age could further the purposes of my life. Finally, the prospect of taking the risk and actually flying a glider fills me with terror. I'm quite certain that I would crash and, if not kill myself, break every bone in my body.

In other words, when it comes to learning hang gliding, my response will always be an unqualified "No way!"

of active participation are present and can be as simple as imagining yourself doing or knowing whatever is witnessed. This, in turn, is related to a degree of risk-taking, because one can be an active participant only by having a go at whatever is being demonstrated.

In the previous chapter, Trish Candia and her kindergarten students typify engaged learners, active participants who wholeheartedly see themselves as meaning-makers. They appreciate and accept their shared role in the demonstration: to make sense of the story being told. Their mission fuels the idea of reader-as-thinker. This venture in working their way to meaning was doable, meaningful, and joyful.

As we begin to tease out what engagement is, it's helpful to clearly articulate what it *isn't*. Many terms are often used interchangeably with *engagement*. In the first-person, real-world example on the previous page, Brian explores the differences between *interest, motivation*, and *engagement*.

Engagement in the classroom is often described in terms of a student's outward behaviors, such as sitting still, eyes looking at the teacher, and not talking. This is more accurately labeled *compliance*, something one does because of an external pressure; learning may not be occurring. This is not Engagement.

Engagement is also not *entertainment*. Students may be entertained by something, such as a cartoon or a movie or even puzzles or word games (or hang gliding), and we say they are engaged. Although students may be entertained by something observed, entertainment's goal isn't necessarily learning.

Engagement is also not the same as *motivation*, which is typically something external that causes us to behave in certain ways. External motivations—such as rewards, grades, or pleasing others—can indeed motivate some students to "learn" something in the short term. But they're not enough to sustain Engagement. Once the rewards, grades, or those other people (including the teacher) are removed from the situation, the learning, if we can truly call it that, fades (Kohn, 2018).

Thinking about Our Own Meaning-Making
• **Think about your daily instruction. What routines, behaviors, and language do you use to support Engagement?**

The Engaged Brain

According to Frank Smith (1975), just as the lungs are the organ of breathing, so the

More to the Story
Why Learning May Not Occur–Recognizing Disengagement

Hallmarks of Disengagement (students may exhibit any or all of these indicators)	Examples of what is often confused with Engagement
• May observe demonstrations with interest and awe but have no desire to learn the act or use the artifact personally	• When students experience something "fun" but don't understand the inherent connections or importance of what is being demonstrated
• May attempt an act or use an artifact but abandons effort easily or quickly	• When students read in school but don't choose to read outside of school, even when texts are available
• May not desire or see a need or purpose to learn what was demonstrated	• When students ask, "Do we need to know this for the test?" or "How will I use this in my life?"
• May engage in an act or use an artifact because of an external motivator	• When students are offered rewards or do something to please a teacher or parent or to "join the crowd
• May experience success in early attempts, but this success is insufficient to sustain the desire to learn more	• When students are rewarded with points for reading certain books

brain is the organ of learning. By this, he means that people are always learning, just as they are always breathing. We just can't help it. When we are awake, our brains are constantly working, processing the data that comes in through our senses. The stream of data is constant, like a flow of water from a tap that can't be shut off. Throughout the constant stream of stimulation coming in from our senses, however, our brains make decisions about what to attend to and what to ignore; otherwise, we would be in meltdown from this onslaught of sensory stimulation.

Take a moment from reading this text, and notice all that has occurred—or is occurring—as you read this chapter. Perhaps there is street noise, or birds singing, or the hum of the air conditioner or refrigerator—maybe you hear all these sounds together. Your brain has registered each and every one of the noises, hums, and various other auditory sensations, but it has chosen not to engage with them. Your attention has been given to what is currently engaging and important—the ideas revealed and exposed within this text. Those choices about what deserves attention are decisions your brain makes to enable you to learn.

We intentionally structure our lives to make this discernment of what's important easier and more likely to occur. During important personal discussions,

More to the Story
Our Discerning Brains

An easy way to recognize what is filtered by one's brain is to watch a video filmed in a classroom. Doors slamming, children laughing, chairs scraping, children gesturing, pencils tapping, children talking, heaters blowing—these everyday movements and ambient noises occur routinely yet barely register in our thinking (until they reach some personal threshold of intolerance!). Every movement and noise, however, will be equally and clearly recorded on a video. Cameras and microphones do not function like our brains; they do not discern between what is important and unimportant when it comes to competing for our attention.

we turn off the television, move away from other conversations, and shift our gazes to our conversational partner(s), ready to heed the words spoken and capture the meanings unspoken. In professional learning sessions, we turn our phones and computers to silent (or off), which allows us to purposefully disengage from the distractions of technology so that we can focus our attention on the content at hand. In our personal spaces, we fill the background with white noise to aid sleeping, or perhaps turn on television or music to accompany us while we clean or cook. But merely regarding any such noise as "background" relegates it to non-attention status because the noise functions simply to make it easier to attend to something else.

Engagement positions us to attend to particular actions or artifacts (or both simultaneously) we deem worthy of notice and/or attention. We decide what to attend to from this mix of actions and artifacts, separating these from the flood of potential demonstrations that could trigger our brains to "fire" (causing a distraction). It's as if the brain spotlights those parts of a demonstration that are relevant to our desired learning. This helps us make sense of the world. We attend only to demonstrations that we deem worthy because they are important to our purposes in learning.

Learning, as we detailed in Chapter 4, begins with a demonstration in an ecological setting appropriate for what is to be learned. Effective demonstrations must be whole enough for the learner to understand the relationships between various parts within the demonstration. While teachers may emphasize certain aspects for learning, it's the learners who determine what part of the demonstration garners their attention. For example, when children hear their father say, "Pass the butter, please," a six-year-old and a two-year-old may attend to completely different aspects of what they heard. While the father's intention was to obtain butter, he also modeled using the word *please*. The six-year-old may attend to the grammar, noting that *please* may occur after the request, instead of before; the two-year-old may notice the intonations and cadences in the word *butter*, repeating the word for himself over and over. This wide discrepancy in attention demands that learner-talkers rely on continual access to multiple demonstrations in which such relationships are embedded. This is true for both oral and written language.

Thinking about Our Own Meaning-Making

• **What in your learning setting or instruction causes distractions for learners?**

• **How might you support learners to discern what to attend to and what to ignore?**

The Engaged Brain in the Constructivist Classroom

As we discussed in Chapter 2, a school setting is different from a home setting or the world in general in relation to learning. In a school setting, we are in the unique position of *intentionally* trying to make learning occur, not just waiting for a child's brain to randomly discover or notice school content. Our time with students is limited, and our content is wide-reaching. The specific collection of ideas in our subject areas—be it literacy, math, science, or history—the ideas we want our students to learn, is predetermined and deemed necessary by someone other than the learner, another challenge to the brain. In a school setting, we don't have the luxury of hoping our students' brains will decide that our subject matter is something they want to learn. So, what do we do to encourage our student's brains to want to learn what we are demonstrating?

Because school learning is so essential to life-long learning, it is crucial we try to create learning settings that capitalize on or capture the alert mode of students' brains. While we acknowledge that we can't precisely *replicate* the learning settings for learning-to-talk or learning-to-ride-a-bike or learning-to-tie-a-shoe, which vary for individual learners, we can *simulate* the general conditions that operate in these learning settings. To this end, in a classroom with large numbers of students, we have to plan to provide multiple opportunities for students to witness whole, complete demonstrations of what is to be learned with ample time and space to make approximations. Within these demonstrations and approximations, we direct students' focus, either subtly or explicitly, to what it is we deem necessary and important for learning. The brain, as Smith stated, is always engaged in learning, always in alert mode. Not only must educators focus the learner's brain on *what* there is to learn within the school setting, they must also illustrate *why* and *how* this learning is important for deep engagement to occur. Planning to provide such opportunities for children to witness these holistic demonstrations is a teacher's reason for being. It takes intentionality, commitment, and sensitivity on a teacher's part to support learners as they choose to engage with certain parts of demonstrations.

So, what makes certain parts of demonstrations worthy of Engagement? Why does a learner choose to attend to some things but not others? And what are intentional teaching decisions we can make to increase the degree to which students are likely to engage with our demonstrations of math, science, history, reading, writing, and so on? These questions guide the next part of our discussion.

What Are Principles of Engagement?

Choosing what gets our attention, and what doesn't, during any demonstration can be explained by the presence or absence of certain principles of Engagement, each of which emerged from Brian's classroom data. When these principles are embedded in a learning setting, the depth of Engagement increases. Brian's data strongly suggest that, when teachers deliberately embed these principles in the classroom discourse, they nurture a learning culture that promotes and supports deep Engagement by learners. Through a Discourse of Meaning-Making—a mix of language, behaviors, beliefs, and values—a culture of learning comes to pervade and saturate the classroom setting, strengthening the Condition of Engagement. Without the presence of the principles of Engagement, even well-structured demonstrations and experiences, from well-intentioned and well-prepared teachers, aren't likely to result in learning.

The principles of Engagement include the following:

❋ *Learners see themselves as "doers" of the behavior in which they are immersed.* Deep engagement with immersions and demonstrations are more likely to occur when children believe they are readers and writers, mathematicians and scientists, historians and engineers (or believe they are capable of becoming any of these).

✷ *Learners understand how our demonstrations are important to their lives.* They regard what we are demonstrating as meaningful and relevant, which makes them more likely to engage with our immersions and demonstrations.

❋ *Learners believe they aren't risking physical or psychological harm by attempting the behavior.* They trust they can make attempts, even those that are incomplete or imperfect, without being penalized in some way.

✷ *Learners like, trust, respect, and want to emulate the person demonstrating.* They benefit from positive and trusting relationships with the teacher and the other students in the classroom.

Principles of Engagement in Action

In a third-grade classroom, a group of lively eight-year-olds formed a circle on the rug. Throughout an hour-long experience, the group talked in whole-class conversations; moved into groups of twos, threes, and fours to explore, discuss, and revise thinking; then turned back to whole-class discussion for more sharing. The students recorded independently in their journals, returned to smaller teams, then came back to whole-class mode. During the lesson, all these groupings occurred several times over, with ongoing movement and talk throughout.

Their task? To cause a small lightbulb, about the size of those found on a string of Christmas tree lights, to light up using only a battery and wires, and then to explain to their classmates how this happens. Their teacher, Jeralyn Johnson, monitored progress as she moved from group to group, layering in academic vocabulary as warranted, probing the students' thinking based on their comments. With Jeralyn's encouragement, students began to share initial unsuccessful attempts. As the experiments continued, all groups eventually succeeded in causing the bulb to light up. Throughout this process, individual students reported group findings by sharing attempts, both successful and unsuccessful, recorded in their science logs. Students used both drawings and words to convey their findings, using a document camera to project their log pages for all to see. As students shared their logs, each donned an oversized lab coat emblazoned with an embroidered label: *Scientist*.

There came a moment when Jeralyn wanted to add an additional tool, a circuit board, to the students' scientific explorations. She asked for their attention and began to demonstrate: "This is a circuit board. Let me show you—" at which point a young scientist named Jorge enthusiastically interrupted her: "Don't tell us! Let us figure it out!" Jeralyn smiled, nodded, and stopped her modeling, as the teams turned back into small groups and began to investigate and incorporate the newest device into their exploration.

Hands-on, exploratory experiences with students are common in today's classrooms. Structures to manage the movement and ensure that all students participate are designed and employed in most classrooms. Social–emotional learning activities and experiences through which students work in teams and share their work occur regularly in many schools. So, what is it that elevates the learning opportunities in Jeralyn's classroom to make Engagement, and learning, more likely to occur?

More to the Story
What Engagement Is *Not* in This Classroom

What we don't see in this classroom is *compliance*, which involves students doing things to please the teacher or show her how smart they are, even though Jeralyn is evidently pleased with their progress.

This lesson isn't designed with *accountability to the teacher*, which involves students following the teacher's directions to complete the task—and makes them see learning as something they do for the teacher.

This exploration is not about *entertaining the students* with a fun activity that excites and interests students but doesn't necessarily construct durable understandings.

This lesson is definitely not about students *being obedient*, which involves being motivated by external controls on their behavior, because, in this classroom, there are no behavior management charts or other digital tools to track student points for participation. Student behavior is physically dynamic and purposeful.

Looking Closely at the Teaching Decisions

The instruction in Jeralyn's classroom nurtures all the Conditions of Learning, including Engagement. Jeralyn created a culture in which students behave as scientists so that they genuinely *think* as scientists. Her expectations of, and responses to, learners provide clear-cut goals for and feedback on their processes. Multiple, planned opportunities transpire across the days and weeks in this classroom for exploring, recording, talking, approximating, sharing, thinking, and rethinking; this leads to students who are comfortable sharing their thinking and approximations with others. These planned immersions and demonstrations of thinking and talking well occur across disciplines. Effective structures for whole-group, small-group, and independent work and sharing afford students opportunities to be responsible for their own learning.

In this classroom, the teacher sees her role as that of a facilitator and guide for the learning experiences. This belief directly affects the teaching decisions she makes. The instructional community this teacher has built hinges on the idea that learners co-construct understandings. The classroom is dialogic in nature, meaning the students use talking with others as a basic tool for learning. This belief leads the teacher to design learning experiences with built-in opportunities for students to use social experiences as tools for extending meanings.

The teacher makes thoughtful, intentional, deliberate teaching decisions on *when*, *where*, and *how* to provide content knowledge, define academic vocabulary, and ask high-level questions. Instead of merely providing vocabulary and ideas prior to this learning experience, Jeralyn's input is contextualized within lessons.

In the earlier lesson with the third graders, for example, during her pre-lesson preparation, Jeralyn created a number of sticky notes, writing one key content vocabulary word per note. After students had completed a number of experiments with their materials, one student illustrated a completed circuit on the whiteboard. Jeralyn then layered in new content vocabulary by labeling the student's drawing with the vocabulary sticky notes. Up to that point, the students had used mostly common, everyday language rather than academic vocabulary. This process enabled students to incorporate the academic vocabulary easily because they were already familiar with the science content under study. In this way, vocabulary was contextualized *within* the lesson.

This teacher's work is responsive to the learners, which is possible only because Jeralyn has considered her learners, situations in which challenges might arise, and what possible supports she might provide if those challenges occur. She does not plan to prevent those challenges, however, by controlling too much. Jeralyn recognizes that "intellectual unrest" precedes learning (personal communication between Brian Cambourne and Donald Graves, 1982), when things aren't always clear yet haven't reached a level to cause frustration or anxiety. Typically, this unrest is a precursor to deeper engagement and problem solving.

Thinking about Our Own Meaning-Making

- **How might you design instruction that encourages moments of "intellectual unrest" to occur?**

- **How might you support students to make the best use of these moments of "intellectual unrest" in your classroom?**

Teaching Decisions Leading to Engagement

The teaching in Jeralyn's classroom may appear to be in the moment, but it might be more accurately described as "planned opportunism" (Johnston, 2012). As we look more closely at the lesson observed and unpack more of the teaching decisions being made, there is much transpiring to support the principles of Engagement.

Let's unpack these principles of Engagement and consider the decisions a teacher makes to honor each.

Learners See Themselves as "Doers" of the Behavior

How we treat ourselves and how others treat us is central to developing our sense of self. Being able to see yourself as someone who does, or is capable of doing, "something" is a key factor in terms of engagement with that "something." As we engage in a behavior   a complete version of a behavior—we come to envision ourselves as a potential "doer" or "knower." By *complete* or *whole* version, we mean a full experience, not smaller, broken-down subparts or elements of that behavior. For example, when riding a bike, we don't learn about pedals, handlebars, and wheels before we actually learn what riding a bike really is.

Whether it's seeing oneself as a reader, a scientist, a golfer, or cook, engaging in a realistic version of this event, even if it's a junior version, is crucial to developing a sense of self as a doer of the whole behavior. David N. Perkins (2009) refers to this as "learning by wholes." Perkins, as we discussed earlier in Chapter 4, cautions against "elementitis," an empty learning of parts and pieces. He also cautions against "aboutitis," a not-very-interesting, seemingly endless learning about something before *doing* what we are learning. These common ways of teaching inhibit learning, because one truly experiences what it means to be a doer of what is being learned by doing it.

In Jeralyn's group of third graders, the students *were* scientists who engaged in the scientific process of exploration, experienced hypotheses being posed, experimented to figure out the efficacy of ideas, and revised a sense of these ideas based on experimentation. The process they applied was central to developing and expanding their view of themselves as learners. Flexible thinking and the ability to persevere can't be directly taught or only requested at testing time; those traits develop only through experiences that encourage this flexibility and perseverance. Jeralyn's decisions to use time, resources, and structures in this manner give space for being productive and proficient learners.

Messages we receive from significant others—parents, teachers, or others we've bonded with—also affect our ability to see ourselves as doers. As Jeralyn responds to students' processes, she communicates a clear belief in the students' capabilities. For example, nodding as students talk demonstrates she takes their thoughts seriously. As she probes their thinking, she demonstrates a desire to understand their ideas completely. She respects their need to explore to figure things out, rather than demanding the students just sit quietly during an unwanted demonstration; in this, she demonstrates her confidence in their abilities to learn. Teachers respond every day to students in ways that shape the students' views of themselves as learners. Becoming more aware of the effect of our actions and words on how learners view themselves increases our impact on their learning.

Becoming more aware of the effect of our actions and words on how learners view themselves increases our impact on their learning.

When we view our "ways of being" in classrooms as opportunities to support each student's ever-developing sense of self as a learner, we broaden our sense of the purpose of instructional strategies. No longer are they just about comprehension or content or practicing skills. Read aloud, shared reading, guided reading, and independent reading become "threshold experiences" (Perkins, 2009), opportunities for actually doing what readers do, which is thinking and talking about a text. In addition, independent reading, followed by a reflection on the experience, becomes an opportunity to increase student agency and competence. This is how we move from doing instructional strategies to using instructional strategies in purposeful ways.

Our instructional decisions matter. From how we talk with students to how we design lesson experiences, we affect the way learners view their abilities to be doers of the very thing they are learning about.

> ### *Mismatch between Theory and Practice*
> ### Responding to Struggling Students' Attempts
>
> Richard L. Allington (2006) cites numerous studies documenting differences in responses offered by teachers to those they deem "struggling" readers and those they consider "proficient." And those differences are dramatic. Teachers are more likely to ask struggling students to read aloud, then quickly interrupt them when they deviate from the text being read, most often telling them to sound out the word.
>
> Contrast this with what teachers are more likely to do and say with proficient readers. Proficient readers are asked to read silently, expected to self-monitor and self-correct, interrupted only after a wait period or at the end of a sentence, and then asked to reread or cross-check.
>
> These differences not only negatively affect the strategic actions of struggling readers but also prevent them from experiencing self-driven successes and developing a sense of self as a doer. So, if we want students to be problem finders and problem solvers in reading, we must coach them as though they're the proficient readers we want them to become.

> ### Thinking about Our Own Meaning-Making
>
> • **How do you support learners to see themselves as "doers" of what you're teaching?**

Learners Understand How These Demonstrations Are Important to Their Lives

Learning by wholes surrounds us every day. "One never knows when one is going to get ambushed into learning something" (Perkins, 2009). What separates learning by wholes from much of school learning is that learners view the endeavors as meaningful, worthwhile, and purposeful. Project-based learning experiences—currently the driving force behind many innovative schools, especially high schools—are built on this kind of learning. But, even within regular, everyday elementary schools, in regular, everyday lessons, the decisions a teacher makes affect each student's sense of purpose. When a teacher uses structures such as turn and talk during learning experiences, students develop their abilities to understand how to learn from others. As teachers facilitate student thinking by asking questions like "What are you thinking?" and "What makes you think that?" learners come to understand that the purpose of what happens in school is to *think*.

As we take seriously the work our youngest learners undertake, purpose permeates the classroom and, in turn, affects the beliefs of each learner. In constructivist classrooms, learners self-monitor their efforts, understanding what they are doing and why, and progress toward goals with an aura of respect and shared purpose (Nichols, 2006). Teachers who are clear in their purpose help shape learners who are more likely to understand that demonstrations are important to their lives.

While making the bulb light up was the aim for the students in Jeralyn's class, the learners understood that the process of figuring out how to make the bulb light up was equally important (and maybe even more so for their future learning experiences). Their sense of accomplishment and ability to gauge their own learning came through their interactions, not just from the bulb being lit. As the students worked in teams, the interactions were valued for how they supported every learner involved, not just what each individual took from the experience. As the teams shared their failed attempts, their means of learning was deemed purposeful by all. In addition, the students were willing to let the teacher know when she was about to interfere with their learning process if she demonstrated something they felt perfectly capable of figuring out on their own. This action demonstrates how the learners have internalized the importance of thinking for oneself and with one's fellow learners. As Peter Johnston (2012) reminds us, "The adult is not the only teacher in the room."

Teachers who are most successful in implementing Conditions of Learning ultimately abandon the idea that teaching is about bits and pieces that will eventually add up to a whole *something*. Instead, the instruction begins with learners collaborating and jointly constructing the meaning of what is to be learned and then unpacking how the bits and pieces work together within the whole. For example, when a teacher chooses to read aloud and discuss meaningful texts in multiple sessions with students—texts like *The Other Side* (Woodson, 2001) or, as

Every interaction with students is an opportunity to be purpose-driven.

noted subsequently in this book, *Pezzettino* (Lionni, 1975) and *The Summer My Father Was Ten* (Brisson, 1998)—learners understand how thinking deepens as we engage with a text multiple times. Our classrooms don't have to be perfect models of the most innovative new structures in education for us to affect how our learners perceive our demonstrations as meaningful. Every interaction with students is an opportunity to be purpose-driven.

Thinking about Our Own Meaning-Making

• **Do your students see what you're teaching as purposeful?**

• **Why or why not?**

Learners Believe They Aren't Risking Physical or Psychological Harm by Attempting the Behavior

Think back to being a student: When the teacher asked a question and you knew the answer, what did you do? And, if you didn't know the answer, what did you do? This pattern of participation is highly documented, a default pattern of classroom discourse known by its own initials—IRE, for initiate, respond, evaluate (Cazden, 1988). We've all experienced the pattern as students, and perhaps even facilitated it as teachers. It goes like this: The teacher "initiates" the exchange with a question. Students indicate that they know the answer with a raised hand (or a downward gaze and slumping posture if they don't). The teacher selects a student to "respond." Then the teacher "evaluates" whether the given answer is correct. This pattern can occur even when teachers ask open-ended questions. They might evaluate a student response by gauging the correctness of the answer ("Close, but not quite" or "You're getting closer . . . ") before moving on to other students. The IRE pattern can also occur in classrooms using dialogic structures, such as turn and talk, when teachers hear from partnerships and evaluate whether or not the responses are correct.

In Jeralyn's third-grade classroom, the community supported each learner's attempts in the experiments. Students recognized the importance of their learning process, not just the product, because their teacher facilitated in ways that signaled her belief in this process. When questions arose, she didn't simply answer; she, instead, turned the questions back to the groups. When a student shared a response, the teacher asked more of the student who had responded ("Say more about that") rather than moving on to engage another student or group, thus giving the student time and space in which to expand on his or her thinking. Students determined what they would share from their learning logs, with whom, and when they would do so. And the youngster who "interrupted" the teacher's modeling with "Don't tell us!" did so knowing his behavior would be accepted by the teacher.

In his blog, *Granted, and . . .* , the late, great Grant Wiggins recounted a high school learning coach's experiences as she shadowed a student through his learning day (Wiggins, 2014). After spending a day alongside a student, the coach, Alexis, reflected that, as a student, "You feel a little bit like a nuisance all day long," being told to be quiet and pay attention repeatedly. She also observed how often sarcasm and snark, impatience and annoyance infused teacher responses to learners. Such responses don't help learning; instead, they create barriers to a positive psychological state for learning. Most learning takes place in an atmosphere of quiet confidence and relaxation (Smith, 1975).

Sometimes, the psychological harm comes from focusing on what students *aren't* doing. In her powerful memoir of a year with her kindergarten class, *The Girl with the Brown Crayon* (1997), Vivian Gussin Paley offers a powerful model of a reflective and responsive teacher. Yet, even this astute teacher felt she had made a student feel inadequate by focusing more on what he couldn't do than on what he was able to accomplish.

Paley's memoir reflects on the learning she and the students took on, as Leo Lionni's picture books, with their mice characters, became touchstone texts during her final year of teaching. In one poignant chapter, she reflects on Walter, a student whose native language is Polish; he sits at the edge of the rug, rarely speaking during whole-group time. In this classroom, children regularly dictate stories to Paley, then illustrate and act out the stories, inviting classmates to become characters in their dramatizations. When Paley asks Walter to dictate a story or paint a picture, he tells her, "I not can it."

While Walter regularly listens and interacts with other students, he chooses not to interact with Paley. She knows Walter is a fluent reader and writer in Polish; he reads books sent by his grandparents and writes them thank-you letters. While Walter is literate in Polish, he judges himself as inadequate when comparing himself to English-speaking students, who are "confident speakers and mouse painters." Walter, it turns out, repeatedly draws squares, reinforcing what Paley believes Walter sees as "daily proof that he cannot draw as well as the others, a burden he adds to his general self-doubts as an English speaker."

Late in the school year, the students read *Pezzettino* (1975). In this book, Lionni uses colored squares and patterns of colored squares to represent characters, rather than the mice characters the students are familiar with. When a fellow student recognizes and celebrates the artistic similarity between illustrations in this particular Lionni book and the squares Walter draws over and over in his notebook, Paley is floored. His classmates perceive Walter's artistic integrity; she has not. She values a dictated story that Walter fends off "as if I am leading him into a trap." She wonders if, by not properly appreciating what Walter *is* offering, his colorful squares, *she* is responsible for his hesitancy and reluctance to share his stories. Perhaps she hasn't truly valued, through her words and her attention, Walter himself.

[Not finding value in what children are able to do can create an unsafe space for learners.] As educator Tina Haselius, in a personal correspondence to the authors (2019), noted, "Our responses to students—how both what we do say as well as what we leave unsaid—can create a lack of emotional safety for our students." These are spaces where learners feel they can't possibly be successful. Sometimes it's what we *don't* do that matters.

A Postscript about Walter

Not long after *Pezzettino* became "Walter's book," and Walter's artistic squares became a point of community pride, Walter began to write a large word over and over again in his notebook. That word was *WLADYSLAW*. This, Walter shared, is his Polish name. With this word, his name, Paley felt Walter was not only showing her a piece of himself but also offering her a piece of *herself*, a "piece I am missing" (Paley, 1997).

Thinking about Our Own Meaning-Making

• **In your classroom, how do you intentionally create emotional safety for learners?**

Learners Like, Trust, Respect, and Want to Emulate the Person Demonstrating

Effective classrooms are filled with learners and teachers. The plurals on both those words are intentional. In effective classrooms, the *learners* include both the children and the adults in the room; so do the *teachers.* Demonstrations are not just initiated by the adults in the room. Students are likely to be showing other students how things work or go in these classrooms (Johnston, 2012).

"Well-formed ideas and intentions amount to little without a community to bring them to life" (Peterson, 1992). Children are learning about literacy and math, science, and social studies, certainly, in our classrooms, but they're also developing theories about coping, managing, and flourishing within a community unlike any other. They're learning about how this place called school and this space called the classroom function. They're coming to terms with their own places in these special environments.

Learners reflect the tone and the language of the classroom as they grow their perceptions of what is acceptable in this space. Their social and emotional understandings are intertwined with their academic understandings. They learn this from interactions with both the adults and the other children (Johnston, 2012); in the process, they develop a sense of trust and respect for all the learners in the classroom, including themselves.

In this two-way learning process, adult teachers notice and name how students are developing within this evolving environment, making adjustments to structures, groups, and demonstrations in response to their observations. They gauge the learning trajectories for each individual learner, developing confidence and trust in their own observations of students along the way (Cambourne, 1988). As teachers make decisions about and for their learners, they reveal themselves to be leaders who hold themselves accountable in how they do their work. Those who lead in these ways rely on their beliefs as a guide to ensure their instruction is aligned with their goals (Sinek, 2009). This consistency in beliefs and actions inspires trust with their learners and, ultimately, trust with themselves.

In the third-grade classroom we visited earlier in this chapter, the interactions among the students and with Jeralyn epitomize a setting that is both built on trust and continuing the ongoing work to nurture trust. The structures she put into place for talking and sharing as a way to learn enabled a sense of trust and respect to thrive. The students sit in a circle, which makes it possible for all students to make eye contact with one another. In the circle formation, students are more likely to hear and respond to comments made by peers and Jeralyn. The back-and-forth use of the whole-group/small-group/whole-group structure offers all students (and Jeralyn) opportunities to have their voices and ideas heard within the group; the configuration sends a clear message that all thinking matters in this community of learners.

Placing value on approximations, as when learners shared the unsuccessful attempts recorded in their science logs, indicates a teacher's belief in the role of such approximations in learning. This, in turn, leads to students' confidence in their own ability to succeed. When their teacher respected the learners' desire to figure out things on their own and turned the responsibility for their learning back to them, her trust in the students as learners was evident. Only when individuals can trust the group to support them, both practically and emotionally, will they be willing to take the risks necessary to advance the culture as a whole; in this case, trust in the group's support allows the individuals to take the risks necessary for independent learning to occur (Johnston, 2012; Sinek, 2009; Peterson, 1992).

Thinking about Our Own Meaning-Making

• **Think about the relationships you have with your students. Which support Engagement?**

• **What have you done to develop that relationship?**

• **Which relationships might need further work?**

• **What might you do to develop that relationship?**

Conclusion

Engagement is necessary for any learning to occur. This is different from compliance, entertainment, interest, or motivation. By seeing themselves as potential doers or knowers of what is being demonstrated, learners make meaning of the observed behavior. Built on a desire within the learner, Engagement requires active participation with what is being learned. Caring relationships within the learning setting are crucial for this Engagement and, therefore, learning.

Hallmarks of Engaged Learners

- Desires to be able to do what is being observed
- Actively participates
- Imagines oneself successfully doing or knowing whatever is witnessed
- Is prepared to take risks
- Attempts whatever is being demonstrated
- Desires to engage with other learners

The potential for Engagement as described in this chapter is greater when the Conditions of Expectation, Responsibility, Employment, Approximation, and Response are nurtured by teachers in classrooms. The next chapter examines these Conditions in depth and offers examples of classroom practice for each Condition.

Thinking about Our Own Meaning-Making

• Think of a moment in a classroom when you recognized that students were engaged in what was being learned. What were the signs?

• What intentional teaching decisions were made that supported Engagement to occur?

• How do you intentionally construct learning settings to support Engagement?

• What mismatches exist between your theory of learning and the ways you support Engagement?

• What other big ideas are you holding as you reflect on this chapter?

• What questions do you have?

"Life is permeated with possibility at every instant. What
distinguishes one life from another is intention, the one thing that we can control."
——Paul Hawken, *Blessed Unrest: How the Largest Movement in the World Came into Being
and Why No One Saw It Coming*

Chapter 6

Conditions That Increase
the Probability of Engagement:
Expectation, Responsibility, Employment,
Approximation, and Response

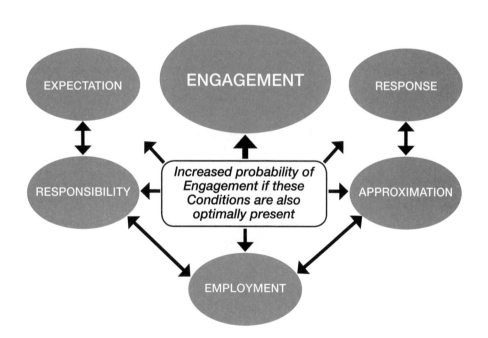

*Blessed Unrest: How the Largest Movement in the World Came into Being and Why No
One Saw It Coming* (2007) is environmentalist, author, and activist Paul Hawken's
exploration of the worldwide intersection of movements in environmentalism, social
justice, and the preservation of indigenous cultures. In the eye-opening account,

Hawken describes an activity he facilitated at a company that produces agricultural chemicals. Through the activity, he hoped to encourage the company's employees to appreciate and understand the practicality and/or necessity of ecologically friendly practices. The two-hour task for the teams of engineers and corporate managers was to "design a spaceship that could leave earth and return in one hundred years with the crew alive, healthy, and happy." In addition to addressing the physical needs of this biome's inhabitants, the design needed to address ideas for the entire culture of their society while providing for their intellectual, social, and emotional necessities. (The guidelines for the activity also stipulated, "what happened on the spaceship stayed on the spaceship" for the entire century!)

Despite various sophisticated proposals, the winning designers' presentation stood out because of some unusual features. The first was the plan to bring along artists, musicians, actors, and storytellers; they would *create* a culture that would help the crew members endure the long journey. This approach seemed highly preferable to relying on canned entertainment, such as movies and musical recordings. In addition, the designers and engineers would bring along weeds, not just useful seeds, because weeds "enliven the soils" by providing much-needed nutrients and interesting biological variety. The designers and engineers also chose to bring along some things, such as bacteria and insects, that skeptics considered to be undesirable. The winning participants, however, saw the inherent value of those additions in an ecosystem. Ultimately, every element that was included served a specific purpose in terms of the sustainability of the ecosystem.

Ironically, those designers and engineers chose to leave behind everything their own company produced because of the effect the products would have on the delicate, enclosed environment; the chemicals were too toxic to be part of a sustainable ecosystem. When asked to create a sustainable world, this winning team envisioned a diverse ecosystem, one with a socially just and equitable society that used only what existed in nature and could be reused and built upon. Those designers and engineers envisioned an organic environment that considered the authentic needs and desires for all its inhabitants.

Envision for a moment a classroom as an ecosystem—a tiny biome that exists for a school year, with the goal of the crew surviving "alive, healthy, and happy." Now, expand that overarching goal to include intellectual, social, and emotional learning. What intentional experiences would we include to create and construct this ecosystem of learning to "enliven the soils"? What would we choose to bring into our learning setting because of its inherent value to learning? What would that classroom environment look like? Sound like? Feel like?

And the even bigger question to consider: What would we deem too "toxic" to be included? What would we stop doing simply because it doesn't support a healthy or happy learning place? What would we leave out to ensure the health and growth of our learners?

Environment. Setting. Climate. Culture. Community. Ecosystem. Each of these terms implies a system of possibilities—with elements that are interactive and intertwined, embedded and ingrained, and unlimited and without boundaries. As teachers and students interact throughout the school days, weeks, and years, they bring their learning ecosystem to life, enlivening its "soils" and nurturing it to its full potential. Resources and processes in the classroom are chosen for their inherent value to learners. Over time, a certain *something* develops; a certain tone, ambience, or atmosphere, a certain *je ne sais quoi*, comes to permeate a classroom where these Conditions are deliberately curated. This tone is enigmatic yet pervasive, almost like the water that surrounds sea life or the air that we breathe. We don't miss it until it becomes toxic or disappears.

In this chapter, we discuss five Conditions of Learning that shape the system of possibilities in a learning setting: Expectation, Responsibility, Employment, Approximation, and Response. When optimally present, these Conditions increase the probability of Engagement. This Engagement, in turn, increases the likelihood of our immersion experiences and demonstrations making a significant difference for learners.

Each of these five Conditions is vital to the success of learners. These Conditions require an intentionality and commitment to ensure their presence. Effective learning spaces are built on an appreciation of how deeply mutual affection and respect influences our learners. These relationships require attention and purposeful nurturing by discerning and deliberate teachers. Also required: an acknowledgment of the pedagogical shifts necessary to align our beliefs and our actions.

> *Effective learning spaces are built on an appreciation of how deeply mutual affection and respect influences our learners.*

Expectation

Expectations involve beliefs about a learner's capabilities, both how learners view themselves and how they are viewed by significant others. Learners are more likely to engage with demonstrations from significant others who hold high expectations for them (Smith, 1983, 1987; Rosenthal and Jacobsen, 1968). The expectations of those to whom learners are bonded are powerful coercers of their behavior. Learners achieve what is expected of them.

Into the Classroom

It's the beginning of center time during the spring in Debra's kindergarten class. The children are actively studying the literacy centers board, a task board or agenda mapping out the various instructional places where small, heterogeneous groups of students will read, write, think, and talk together throughout the morning. While they are engaged in these reading and writing practices, Debra plans to meet with small groups of students in shared or guided reading. Since the groups meeting with her are not indicated on the task board, Debra takes the opportunity to explain her expectations for these specific groups of students.

"Today, I will meet with Justin, Amy, Jorge, and Trinika during the first rotation in centers," Debra says. "Remember, you four will be able to choose whatever center you want after we meet together. Amy, I know you are really excited about going to writing center to make your mom's get-well card. You won't miss that center because we are working together."

"Since James and Shondra are absent today," Debra continues, "I'll wait to meet with their group until tomorrow. So, Christina, Santiago, Cameron, Ashia, and Tyler, we will work together today after your first center. You can choose whatever center you want today in the first rotation."

Returning her focus to the entire group, Debra encourages the students to "take a look at the centers board and think about your plan for this morning." (By this time in the school year, she doesn't go over the board each day, just simply asks students to use the board as a reference.) After the students have a brief talk with their partners about their plan for the morning, Debra asks them, "What thoughts or questions do you still have about your morning?"

While most students move to their centers, several students stay behind to talk about issues they're still pondering. One student, Mariah, isn't sure how to persuade the other students in the listening center to listen to her choice, a recording of "The Gingerbread Man" story. Debra and Mariah practice what to say and how to say it (nicely and without whining). They also discuss a compromise, namely, what Mariah will do if the other students still say no. ("I might have to listen to something else today," Mariah sighs.)

Teaching Decisions Affecting Expectation

As we said earlier, the Condition of Expectation involves both how learners view themselves and how they are viewed by significant others. As described in Chapter 5, on Engagement, learners must see themselves as being capable of learning. This belief, or sense of self, is often signaled through the messages and language significant others, such as parents or teachers, use when communicating with

> *More to the Story*
> **Changing Our Language**
>
> One term used by many teachers, students, and parents regarding students' learning activities and behaviors is the word "work." We believe this is a loaded word that can communicate that school learning is a chore or a laborious task. Instead of saying, "Today we are working on…", perhaps we say "Today we will be thinking about…" But changing our language choices is a challenge as a term such as "work" is deeply embedded in our discourse. Although in this book we use the word "work," we do so only because it is so prevalent. Our intention is to communicate that the "work of learning" is meaningful, can be challenging, but should ultimately be joyful. In Chapter 7, we unpack this language conundrum further.

learners. Learners will more readily respond to or engage with the expectations of someone they respect, like, value, and want to emulate, someone with whom they've bonded.

Learners achieve what they expect to achieve and what others expect of them.

Learners achieve what they expect to achieve (Cambourne, 2001) and what others expect of them. When parents are asked whether they think their child will learn to speak their language, the response is unequivocal: "Of course." When parents consider whether a child will learn to read, the responses become conditional: "If he has a good teacher." Teachers often innocently echo this conditional stance through the language they use. "If only her parents would help at home," "If only we had more time to ___," "If only we had ____," and the list goes on. The caution here is: What is expected of learners can become self-fulfilling.

Expectations shape the way we do everything in a classroom. For example, in the way Debra began independent time, she used an everyday routine to prepare students for a productive and important learning time. The students in this classroom set expectations for themselves within familiar literacy centers: Big Books, Library, Book Boxes (copies of previously read guided reading books), Writing Center, Letter and Word Study, and Listening. The expectations for what might occur and the decisions to be made by the learners within each of the centers had been established early in the school year. As each center was introduced, explained, and discussed, the students and Debra explored what might be accomplished in the time and space afforded for the center and how their work together would help them learn more about reading and writing. For example, in Big Books, there was much discussion and many demonstrations on how to care for books, how many big books might be read during one center rotation, and how rereading books supports a reader. These discussions clearly communicated, explained, and clarified the expectations for the center.

Embedded within each structure and routine is a range of expectations, both obvious and subtle, communicating the purpose for a day's plan and each learner's role in what would occur. These structures and routines help prepare learners to relax and focus on the upcoming reading, writing, thinking, and talking. Debra's calm and welcoming tone and her stance as a listener and fellow problem solver communicated her interest in her students and her belief that they are able to think for themselves. She took their issues and concerns seriously. Teaching in this way illuminates Debra's belief in and her expectations of the students as learners.

At the same time, she personalizes her instruction as she adjusts her expectations for individual students based on her understandings of learning development along a continuum. In literacy, she is aware of each student's development as decoder, comprehender, and language user *over time*. When she began to meet with small groups, Debra created a column in her weekly lesson plans for assessment (an idea she heard Brian speak about earlier in her teaching career) to indicate who and what she intended to assess. In this way, over a period of two or three weeks, she could systematically assess and evaluate all students.

To accomplish this ongoing, formative assessment, three children received large laminated name cards before they moved into center areas. Debra met with these students during cleanup time to hear about their work: the reading, writing, thinking, and talking events in which they had engaged to make meaning. As she handed the cards to the three students, Debra said, "I can't wait to hear what you share with me today," communicating her expectations of them as capable learners.

During the after-centers conferences, Debra used what she knew about each learner to assess their ongoing literacy development. For instance, as one student reads a page from a big book, she might name and note this student's one-to-one match and comprehension. When another student shares the birthday card she made for her mom, Debra names and notes the student's letter–sound correspondence and genre knowledge. For a student rereading a previously read guided reading book, she takes a running record and discusses meanings they have constructed after rereading the book several times. While each student selects what she or he felt best illustrated their day's work, Debra names and notes their ever-evolving literacy skills and strategies and attitudes, validating the idea that learning is a process that takes time and practice. As she focuses on student's approximations, she continually enhances her own expectations of each learner's abilities.

Debra uses clear language, examples, and models of what she expects from her students. She explains not only the *what* and *how* of each lesson, activity, or

More to the Story
Assessment and Expectations

Sherryl Compston, a New Zealand teacher Debra had the privilege of visiting and working with in her classroom, shared the idea of using name cards as a means to gather assessment data from students' independent work. Since the students' independent learning in centers focuses on the process of literacy development, it doesn't typically produce a pencil–paper product. As center rotations begin, up to three children receive a large, oversized card with their first name printed on it. As children read or write in various centers, they decide what to share to highlight the thinking they did. The oversized-so-it-can't-be-missed name card is placed on the text or other "product," signaling it as the work to be shared with the teacher.

When cleanup time begins, these students are excused from cleaning to organize their thinking for a conference with the teacher. The teacher rotates to each student with a name card, pausing for a minute or two, and, as the students share, the teacher takes notes on the important thinking behaviors done by each student. Students' expectations for themselves are revealed as they share their accomplishments. (This same idea can be applied during math time, collecting equivalent data about their math abilities.)

There are two important reasons to indicate who will share *before* independent time begins, both of which relate to expectations. If deciding who will share takes place *after* students have read, written, thought, and talked, students may do independent work for the sake of compliance or because they're afraid they'll be called on afterward. By indicating who will share *before* they begin, students notice their own learning and expectations for themselves and then make decisions about what they believe represents their best efforts. Engagement deepens for learners as they are encouraged to take responsibility for demonstrating their own understandings.

The second reason to indicate who will be sharing *before* students begin their work has to do with trust, another principle of Engagement. If teachers use sharing as a tool to ensure all students are "held accountable," children quickly realize the teacher doesn't trust them to be learners. Expectations are not about holding children accountable.

structure but also the *why* behind those elements. Expectations are imperceptibly layered within her behavior and language, increasing the likelihood of Engagement for the learners.

Debra's intentional language accomplishes two important things for learners. First, it reveals an expectation that the learners are capable of thinking deeply about what they are learning. She believes in them, and her language communicates her sense of trust in the learners *as learners*. As she acknowledges choices they are free to make before and after they meet with her, students are clear on what decisions to make. Through her phrasing of questions (i.e., "What words might you use to help the other children want to hear the story again?" and "What questions and thoughts do you have?"), an expectation for thinking is embedded for every student.

Another result of Debra's intentional language: It positions these learners to see *themselves* as capable literacy users whose thinking and questions are important (and normal) learner behavior. Students' expectations of themselves develop through making choices on what will guide their learning. For example, within the after-centers conferences, each learner decides what to share as evidence of his or her learning. Those expectations give purpose to their interactions with texts, other students, and Debra.

In addition, parameters and guidelines for what goes on in the classroom (the what, how, and why) are presented in clear and age-appropriate language. Within those parameters and guidelines, students are able to wonder, question, and share confusions without being judged as confrontational or labeled as "not smart." And, while behavior issues eventually and obviously happen as within any classroom setting, the relationship between Debra and the children allow them to problem-solve whatever issues arise.

More to the Story
Relationships and Behavior Issues

Nothing causes more lost sleep, nightmares, and angst for a teacher than when things don't go smoothly in the classroom—many a teacher conversation focuses on this very topic! Orchestrating "the complex problems of living together" (Peterson, 1992) is no small feat, and issues will arise no matter how long you've taught or how well you understand your content. Some of the stress in these moments, however, can be mitigated by focusing on relationships; one marker of a truly strong relationship is the ability to weather the rough patches. Ralph Peterson states, "Community in itself is more important to learning than any method or technique."

Throughout this book, the examples of teaching we have included exemplify instruction built on a foundation of strong classroom communities. Such communities lie at the heart of a classroom using the Conditions of Learning to guide teaching decisions. Language used by teachers within these classroom examples is intentional. Inherent throughout the professional literature (Vygotsky, 1962; Whorf, 1956; Johnston, 2012) is the idea that language shapes thoughts, feelings, and experiences, producing fundamentally new forms of behavior. Paula Denton, in *The Power of Our Words: Teacher Language That Helps Children Learn* (2007), says skillful teacher language helps students "in three broad ways: developing self-control, building their sense of community, and gaining academic skills and knowledge."

While things may not go smoothly with intentional teaching at first, teaching with an eye toward nurturing relationships is essential so that when issues do arise—and they will—we have something to sustain us in what Peterson (1992) calls "life and learning in a crowded place."

Additional Thoughts about the Condition of Expectation

Expectation as a Condition of Learning requires a particular stance by the teacher, one in which success is measured by students developing a sense of h, "a sense that if they act, and act strategically, they can accomplish their goals" (Johnston, 2004). Offering students opportunities to be successful and then helping them understand how they were successful, or not, encourages learners as they develop the stance, or mindset, of a learner, one that is dynamic and agentive (Johnston, 2012; Dweck, 2006). However, teachers can't just tell a student to have a growth mindset and to be agentive; it must be experienced to take root.

Students who have positive and nonthreatening experiences first, and are helped to see themselves as productive, develop their own abilities to self-initiate, self-monitor, and self-reflect. Having these successful experiences first—*before* encountering appropriately challenging situations—is critical. The challenging situations can then afford learners opportunities to have a "productive struggle" (Pasquale, 2015). "As students engage with a task, they must be mindful about the strategy they employ and assess whether it is productive. When they find they are at a dead end, they must be willing to abandon one strategy for another." However, a defining characteristic of productive struggle implies that students are aware of successful strategies *for themselves* rather than relying on those suggested by the teacher. Expectations lead teachers to provide the demonstrations, time, and opportunities necessary to become agentive. Structuring the classroom thoughtfully and using intentional language to foster learning situations helps learners live in ways that support them to become empowered learners.

A second caution about expectations is this: Learners' belief in themselves can be impeded when someone imparts their own negative beliefs about what is to be learned. This can be intentional or inadvertent. For example, when a teacher, parent, or other student communicates a feeling of fear, inability, or insecurity about what is to be learned, a learner may adopt the same stance in response. If teachers believe math to be "so difficult," if parents believe swimming to be "too dangerous," if other learners believe writing to be "too hard"—these beliefs can be adopted by other learners. The same is true when learners are pigeonholed by labels—the "slow" group, the "intervention" group, the "below-grade-level" group, the "low" group.

Messages about expectations, often subtle, are communicated through the structures put into place and the language used. The Condition of Expectation underpins the ethos of any learning culture, whether home or school or, really, anywhere learning is expected to occur. And, while expectations may sometimes seem intangible or ephemeral, their absence is notable.

Thinking about Our Own Meaning-Making

- **In your classroom, how do you intentionally communicate expectations for your learners?**

- **What expectations do the students have for themselves?**

- **How do these expectations affect Engagement for students?**

Responsibility

Responsible learners need to make their own decisions about why, when, how, and what "bits" to learn in any learning task. Learners denied the opportunity to make such decisions are disempowered.

Into the Classroom

During independent reading time, two kindergarten students approached their teacher, Trish Candia, and stated emphatically, "We're having a problem with our partnership" (echoing the language Trish used during class meetings when discussing other problems). Taking their issue most seriously, Trish asked both students to explain the problem as they saw it. One partner said, "He won't put the book in the middle so I can see the pictures when he reads the book." The second partner said, "Well, I know we're supposed to put the book in the middle, but I can't read the words good when it's in the middle." Trish nodded, agreeing they did indeed have a problem.

Trish routinely guided the class through problem-solving when challenges arose in the classroom, so her next words were familiar to these students: "What can you do to solve this problem?" These words intentionally positioned the two learners to be agentive, putting the responsibility for resolving their problem squarely with the students. "Well . . . um . . . ," one partner began hesitantly, "I could read the page and then put it in the middle so he can see the pictures?" Trish said, "That is one solution you could try." She turned to the other student and asked, "What do you think?" The other partner said, "I think that solution is a good solution for us to try." Trish said, "So, you have one solution to try—one partner reads a page and then puts the book in the middle so the other partner can see the pictures. If that solution works, that's great. If that solution doesn't work, you can think about other ideas to try. And if you need my help again, just let me know. Partners again?" The two young readers nodded eagerly, did a fist-bump, and went back to independent reading.

Teaching Decisions Affecting Responsibility

The philosopher Bertrand Russell advocated for teachers to treat their learners seriously from the beginning, giving them responsibilities, talking to them candidly, and setting them up to be thinkers of significant thoughts. When Trish took the problems of the young partnership seriously, she regarded these students as responsible members of the classroom. The idea that a student is capable of being responsible for things going well, as well as for figuring out what to do when they don't, is central to the learner developing a vision of self as a doer of what is to be learned, a principle of Engagement. Often, educators describe this ability to be responsible as "owning the learning" or "making the learning one's own."

> *More to the Story*
> **On the Conditions Being Synergistic**
> This message attributed to Russell is also applicable to the previously discussed Conditions of Engagement and Expectation, reminding us of the systemic, integrated nature of the Conditions of Learning.

The strategic thinking we do as we problem-solve in non-literacy life experiences is the same kind of strategic thinking we do as learners of oral and written language (Dorn and Soffos, 2005). So effective teachers structure classroom experiences to provide opportunities throughout the day for students to engage in decision-making. For instance, in the story of using name cards to assess, in the section on Expectation, Debra asked students to determine what work they felt best represented their thinking. This expectation communicated her belief in their ability to make decisions and take responsibility for their own learning. Throughout the day, teachers have the power to support students or deny them the experiences necessary to become responsible for their own learning. Encouraging students to make decisions is a key to developing responsibility. Students choose writing topics instead of the teacher specifying topics. They choose their own independent reading texts based on interest instead of someone, or some level, deciding for them. In all learning experiences, the teacher provides constructive responses so students become aware of effective strategies they can apply to new learning situations. Each of these experiences provides opportunities for teachers to demonstrate the types of responses that develop responsible learners.

Another layer of decision-making by learners involves what they attend to during our demonstrations. While learning to talk, learners decide what part, or parts, of a demonstration they attend to and when they attend to a particular language task. For example, consider a language demonstration in the form of a command: "Please put on your sandals." A learner may notice the idea of "sandals" and learn the label for this special type of shoe. Alternatively, another learner may be considering the fuller context of the message, as in, "When I put on my shoes, it's time to go outside." Ultimately, children themselves are responsible for learning to talk—and for applying the most useful understandings from demonstrations—oral, gestural, intonation, etc.—in sync with their own development.

Learning from classroom demonstrations is no different. In classrooms, learners also decide what things they attend to during demonstrations of reading and writing. Teachers help students develop responsibility by assuming they are attending to explicit demonstrations and by acknowledging that learners are constructing their own meanings. Effective teachers also acknowledge and accept when learners attend to different parts of demonstrations than the one the teacher intended. For example, during a shared reading lesson that Debra observed, a student identified the dot on the lowercase letter *i* as a period in the book. His kindergarten teacher noted that these dots do look exactly the same. She accepted his approximation and located a period at the end of a sentence for all the learners to compare to the dot on an *i*. More importantly, the teacher then made explicit her expectation that the student should assume responsibility for self-correcting his thinking. She did this by offering him another attempt to locate a period, which he did. In this way, she preserved the integrity of the learner and the teacher–student relationship, while simultaneously strengthening her demonstration.

The most effective teachers recognize a student's attempts at meaning-making while also honoring the learner's developing abilities, marking the moment with "emphasis, or prolonged attention, sharing the experience" (Clay, 1998). The most effective teaching occurs when demonstrations are timely and relevant, based on

---

More to the Story
But What If They Aren't Taking Responsibility?

The Condition of Response and the Process of Application are closely connected to the Condition of Responsibility. Later in this chapter, in the section on Response, we discuss the idea of "upping the ante," which is when we notice our learners aren't assuming responsibility and decide to ask for more from the learner. In "Upping the Ante," we consider how and when to press students to take on specific skills and strategies we have been explicitly demonstrating. Later, in Chapter 8, "Processes That Empower Learning," the Process of Application also considers how we ask students, explicitly, to try on or have a go at what we are demonstrating.

being attuned to student awareness, when teachers "interact to expand what can be attended to, expanding the teachable moment and the child's opportunity to notice something novel" (Clay, 1998). This kind of teaching honors the learner as responsible and capable, supporting his or her engagement in learning.

Classroom Challenges in Students Assuming Responsibility

Some challenges, however, should be noted in this approach to teaching. First, all this noticing and naming and attending to our learners takes time. It also takes time for students to work through problems for themselves. And it takes patience on our part. Time and patience can challenge even the most dedicated teacher, what with packed schedules, overcrowded classrooms, and never-ending testing! In our efforts to be efficient, we create classrooms to eliminate as many problems as possible, with the goal of everything running smoothly. But, in the name of all this efficiency, we must ask ourselves a question: Are we eliminating too many moments for learning by making decisions for our students, ones they are perfectly capable of making on their own? Affording learners problems to find and problems to solve and giving them time to think and process is key to developing self-regulated and responsible learners. Just as Jeralyn, in Chapter 5, showed us in her lesson, putting aside our own planned demonstration when we realize students don't need it can be the most effective, and time-efficient, teaching.

Affording learners problems to find and problems to solve and giving them time to think and process is key to developing self-regulated and responsible learners.

Another challenge may arise when we consider standards, or learning outcomes. As teachers, we are responsible for students learning particular content, and we may feel concerned some students might never accept the learner responsibilities we want them to assume. If we wait for students to "discover" everything on their own, some students will be at a disadvantage (Delpit, 1995), and some content isn't necessarily "discoverable." Sometimes, a nudge is needed; that is, a kind of explicit teaching where we focus, or refocus, a learner on something we need them to attend to.

For instance, at the beginning of lessons, a teacher's role is to focus students on what aspects of the demonstration are intended for students to notice and practice within the lesson. Unfortunately, many teachers begin by asking, "What have we been learning about. . .?" What happens is inevitable: Students offer guesses, searching back over what has been taught in the past few days, trying to figure out what the teacher wants to hear. More focused teaching language within a lesson introduction would begin something like, "We have been learning about. . . ."

Through this language, a teacher clearly and explicitly articulates the intended link to prior learning. As the teacher layers on new ideas in today's lesson, students are more likely to understand his or her intentions.

> ### *Mismatch between Theory and Practice*
> ### Going over Skills or Strategies before Reading in Guided Reading
>
> In today's educational milieu, various versions of guided reading exist. Some versions ask teachers, in the lesson introduction that occurs before reading, to review what may be problematic for readers or to identify strategies readers should use while reading. When teachers do either of these things, they squander opportunities for students to be responsible meaning-makers.
>
> Before meeting with the students, the teacher is fully responsible for forming groups, determining instructional focuses, selecting texts, and planning lessons. Once the lesson begins, the teacher relinquishes the roles of meaning-maker and problem solver. In guided reading, students assume the roles of problem finder and problem solver as they decide when, how, and why to apply known reading strategies. This meaning-making work is their responsibility.
>
> So what does a teacher working to support student responsibility do in an introduction? Introductions in guided reading lessons support students, with a teacher's guidance, to build story lines or information lines of thinking as they interact with the illustrations, graphics, and words. These discussions integrate vocabulary and language patterns found within the text to activate semantic and syntactic sources of information for students. These meaning- and language-based scaffolds assist novice readers for whom the graphophonic system is just beginning to emerge as a support. Even in these beginning stages of reading, however, observant teachers recognize a need to hold back their responses as students demonstrate more ownership and responsibility for independently reading and understanding the text. And, as teachers work with students in early and fluent stages of reading development, readers are expected to introduce books *to themselves*, with the teacher alongside to support, rather than lead, this book exploration.
>
> When teachers work through problems anticipated within the text before students read the text, they signal that students aren't capable of making meaning for themselves, thereby undermining student responsibility. Guided reading is about meaning-making where the intent is students, with the support of the teacher, reading, thinking, and talking their way purposefully through a text (Ministry of Education, New Zealand, 1985).

Thinking about Our Own Meaning-Making

• **In your classroom, what responsibilities do your students assume for their own learning?**

• **How does this affect Engagement?**

Employment

Learners need time and opportunity to use and practice what has been demonstrated, in order to develop control over their evolving abilities. This use and practice must be functional, realistic, and authentic.

Into the Classroom

*"Do you hear it, Ms. Candia? There's **and** in 'Jack **and** Jill.' Do you hear it?"*

This excited outburst in Trish Candia's kindergarten classroom occurred during daily literacy centers where students chose various texts to read and reread, many of which had been used previously during whole-group instruction (Crouch, 2018). The chart of the nursery rhyme "Jack and Jill" had been read and reread multiple times in various shared reading experiences since the beginning of the school year. This day's independent rereading of "Jack and Jill" was especially important to Cameron, however, because a word the class had read and written and studied in multiple texts throughout the school year—a word that had a prominent place on the students' word wall but had eluded him until that moment—suddenly became visible. That word was *and*. On this particular day, Cameron noticed that word for *himself!* And, on this day, that word became meaningful for *him*.

Teaching Decisions Affecting Employment

Just as children learning to talk require time and opportunity to practice their evolving language, readers and writers require time to use and approximate what they are learning. And, as young learners seem to know intuitively, their practice or employment of language must occur both with others and by themselves. Parents of young children recognize that a child's talk is ongoing. Even when others aren't around or necessarily attending to their talk, children are employing language. (Parents, grandparents, and other adults sometimes share the absolute joys of listening in on a child talking to himself or herself after they've put the child to bed!) By using their developing language skills, children can apply and practice what they are learning about how language works and the various purposes it serves. This practice helps children progress toward fluency in oral language. Learning the print version of language requires this same time and opportunity for practice.

In some classrooms, however, independent time consists of practicing component parts of reading and writing, not actual, meaningful reading and writing. Children in these classrooms experience what we have referred to twice already in this book—they experience "elementitis" (Perkins, 2009), the idea of "week after week, even year after year of focusing on elements" but with little actual reading and writing of extended texts. Students in these classrooms spend their practice time working mostly on skill practice in isolation. "What this does is narrow the door for readers in a way that can give them a warped view of reading—and it prevents us from seeing all they might be capable of" (Vinton, 2017). On her blog, *To Make a Prairie*, Vinton (2020) goes on to say, "My hunch—and my experience—has led me to believe that if we carve out space for students to show us what they're intellectually capable of, many who've been labeled as struggling have incredibly thoughtful and insightful things to say. So let's not underestimate them by narrowly focusing on a diet of skills." This narrow kind of practice can certainly help learners demonstrate skills in isolation, but this isn't the ultimate goal. This kind of practice doesn't translate into readers who have strong comprehension, or confident writers who write strong pieces, or learners who enjoy reading and writing and enthusiastically choose to do both. Skill knowledge is absolutely necessary, but it isn't sufficient on its own to develop strong readers and writers.

Children in many classrooms also spend a great deal of time engaging in what Richard L. Allington calls "stuff" (2006). These are the reading-related kinds of tasks created and developed to keep children busy and occupied while teachers meet with groups or individuals. The tasks are connected to topics and books they have read about together. "Stuff" includes making dioramas, answering questions, completing worksheets, and crafting character webs. Each of these tasks is most

---

Mismatch between Theory and Practice
Using a Reading Notebook as a Substitute Workbook

A reader's notebook can be a powerful tool for supporting readers to trace their reading lives. Students can keep a running log of books read, books to be read, and responses to books that have mattered to them. The reader, with a teacher's guidance, can use the notebook to monitor personal reading preferences, set reading goals, and support conversations about texts. Teachers and students may even use them to dialogue about books read or those being considered.

When reading logs, however, become glorified substitutes for workbooks, they no longer support reading in productive ways. For instance, when a reading notebook involves a writing task to be completed daily, or students are required to write summaries about every book they read—or when students must answer questions about books before, during, and after reading—the distinction between a reading notebook and a workbook can get blurred or, in some cases, obliterated. The notebook has become reading-related "stuff" that doesn't support students to live more readerly lives.

In her book *The Book Whisperer: Awakening the Inner Reader in Every Child* (2009), Donalyn Miller includes a chapter titled "Walking the Walk." In it, she urges teachers to create a reader's notebook, too, as part of a journey to find their own "inner reader." Why? Because, if teachers don't live the readerly (and writerly) lives they are asking students to live, how will they ever have credibility with students?

often assigned as a way to check for understanding, and then, in many cases, the work is graded. Unfortunately, reading logs and other written reactions can also fall into this category of "stuff," depending on how those materials are used. Children whose reading and writing is limited to this kind of practice don't experience the decision-making, the orchestration of strategic thinking, or the flat-out joy involved in meaning-making that leads to lifelong literacy.

The Condition of Employment requires teachers to create daily opportunities in classrooms for genuine reading and writing experiences—this is the point of independent reading and writing times. These experiences can be student-selected, thereby increasing Responsibility and Expectation, both of which strengthen Engagement. Independent reading within a reader's workshop in which students self-select books from the classroom library is an example of this kind of experience.

Mismatch between Theory and Practice
Applying Skills in Isolation

As skill lessons end, teachers typically send students off to "do" something with the skill that has been taught. This application is often some type of sheet to complete or an activity for which students are asked to "apply" the skill. The sheet or activity isolates the skill being studied, for example, asking students to draw a line under a pattern found in multiple examples of words to reinforce identifying that pattern. It may ask them to trace or write a letter repetitively to learn its proper formation or read a book composed with mostly words using a specific phonics pattern to reinforce decoding using that phonics skill. These kinds of independent activities reinforce a view of literacy that favors one source of information, the graphophonic system.

While beginning readers must learn to use this system with automaticity to develop an effective reading process, readers must integrate all three sources of information: semantic (meaning), syntactic (language), *and* graphophonic (phonological). Learners must see demonstrations of how to integrate these systems in "continuous text"—texts with a meaning and language context, that is, sentences, paragraphs, etc. (Parkes, 2000; Clay, 1991). Reading in continuous text allows a reader to access sources of information not available when the reading task emphasizes only letters and words. In continuous text, for example, readers can use context to determine the meaning of a pronoun. They can also use redundancies that occur in continuous texts, such as using an illustration *and* a label on the illustration *and* the word in the sentence itself to understand the meaning of a word. These multiple ways of knowing something within a text are accessible only in the sentences and/or larger passages found in continuous text. Isolated skill worksheets and letter/sound activities can't provide this kind of reading experience and practice.

Applying and integrating all information systems, including letters, sounds, and all the other components of phonics, is necessary to truly develop strategic, independent meaning-makers. The practice of using skills occurs when students read teacher-selected and student-selected continuous texts, applying and integrating all the sources of information as they read.

These encounters can also be teacher-designated, to support students as they apply skills and strategies gleaned from demonstrations. Trish knew that revisiting known big books and charts in a center would offer Cameron ample time and space and choice to practice integrating meaning, structure, and visual systems. Working in a known text holds meaning and syntax steady so emergent readers can figure out how the letters and sounds work, which means their skill work is contextualized within a meaningful reading. What is central to any meaningful practice is the notion of authenticity—the complete experience of meaning-making. This can only occur if students are immersed in complete or whole texts.

Thinking about Our Own Meaning-Making

• **Think about the Condition of Employment related to your own classroom. What opportunities do you provide for authentic practice of what is to be learned?**

• **How do these opportunities affect Engagement?**

Approximation

Learners approximate, or make attempts, when learning and must have the freedom to approximate the desired model. Rather than avoiding "mistakes," learners must understand that these approximations are essential for learning. This freedom, and expectations that mistakes are normal learning behaviors, are critical aspects of a learning culture.

Into the Classroom

A group of lively first graders had been reading and rereading *A Pizza for Bear* (O'Connor, 2017). In this delightful big book, Bear—after consuming berries and honey, being chased by bees, and then swimming to escape those bees—finds himself hungry again. He smells pizza through the trees, surprises some campers, and makes a meal of their pizza. ("Cheese and tomato. Crunch! Crunch! Crunch!") The illustration on the final page shows Bear sauntering off, looking satisfied.

A few days after reading and rereading the book, Debra, their teacher, modeled writing a continuation of the story and then invited the children to do the same, thinking about and detailing what Bear might do next. Partners generated and discussed their "after-the-end" stories, using what they knew about real bears in tandem with imagination to extend the narrative. After talking with partners, they excitedly headed to their tables to write their own approximations, their own "endings," to author Nancy O'Connor's story. The students wrote easily and confidently, approximating language, spelling, and punctuation. Students used a range of strategies to get their ideas onto paper, including talking their stories aloud to themselves, using charts and other print items on the walls, and approximating spelling of some words while relying on a large bank of high-frequency words whose spellings they knew automatically.

More to the Story
Video of Shared Writing Using *A Pizza For Bear*

Video of the lesson described above can be viewed at:
https://www.teachingdecisions.com/shared-reading-returning-to-the-text-modeling-writing/

Teaching Decisions Affecting Approximations

When children are learning to talk, they use a great deal of temporary language, often referred to as baby talk, a stage of learning the oral form of language. Almost everyone is familiar with this concept and can readily supply an example of adorable expressions of this temporary language: *Dat Daddy shoe? Me go ta-ta* (a walk). *Me want binkie* (pacifier). Many parents even record this language in baby books, making an effort to capture exactly what the child said and how she or he said it. (The impulse is to hold memories of the toddler's chatter close to their hearts—or possibly to embarrass their adult child at her or his wedding!) Rarely is anyone concerned that a toddler's language will become a permanent part of the child's repertoire. Responding to the intentions behind children's messages honors their approximations as true and meaningful communication.

Approximations in learning written language and abilities function similarly to a baby's language. We (parents and teachers) celebrate delightful approximations of spelling (i.e., "invented spelling") and made-up readings of familiar stories. Until we don't. Somehow, once children enter school, the demands for "correct" and "complete" become the expectation, while approximations are devalued. This shouldn't be the case. Approximations serve as windows into how children's reading and writing processes are developing. They are windows into student's strategic thinking.

For the aforementioned lesson, after the students completed their after-the-end pieces, Debra studied their writing to observe their approximations (see following page). By doing so, she learned several things that would inform future demonstrations for these first graders. *Sleppe*, *pizzae*, and *sliseis* were examples of invented, or temporary (Cambourne and Turbill, 1987), spellings of the words *sleep*, *pizza*, and *slices* generated by some students in their stories. These spelling examples demonstrated their ability to recognize spelling-as-it-looks, implying attention to graphic patterning or visual memory. Others used approximated, temporary spellings for high-frequency words, such as *owt* for *out* and *sum* for *some*, implying attention to spelling-as-it-sounds or spelling-as-it-sounds-out. Debra noted the need for a series of lessons on using both of these strategic ways to read and write words. These lessons support students to use a variety of encoding strategies to get ideas onto paper, ensuring students move toward conventional spelling.

Debra also noted that some students had attempted dialogue in their illustrations, using speech bubbles, demonstrating an increasing awareness of how characters are revealed by an author and the ways authors incorporate dialogue in a story. This suggested the need for a series of lessons on reasons writers use dialogue as well as on the conventions for including and punctuating dialogue in print.

Additional Thoughts about the Condition of Approximation

How we respond to student's approximations can have a crucial effect on our relationship with our students, which, in turn, affects their engagement. Responding

Mismatch between Theory and Practice
Students Reading Silently versus Students Reading Aloud

Many times during the school day, students are asked to read aloud. Teachers check for decoding with accuracy, correct pronunciation of words, attention to punctuation, and appropriate phrasing. Yes, reading aloud does inform a teacher about those reading components. Some teachers, however, also believe these elements to be signs that students are reading with understanding. Even though fluency and decoding are aspects of reading related to meaning-making, none of these components guarantee students are reading for meaning. In fact, almost every teacher has listened to a student read aloud with perfect accuracy and fluency but not comprehend what was read.

Readers read with divided attention: to print and to meaning. When someone reads aloud, especially in front of peers or an authority figure, the attention is no longer divided—the focus is primarily on making the reading sound good. In other words, performance is paramount. Comprehension is challenging to construct when most of the reader's attention is elsewhere.

Silent reading, on the other hand, offers readers the opportunity to attend to and integrate both print and meaning information (dare we say "undivided attention"), employing reading behaviors necessary to construct, deconstruct, and reconstruct meaning. In the solitude of their own thoughts, readers are free to pause, mispronounce, monitor, reread, and self-correct without judgment from listeners. The approximations they make as they decode and strategically work their way to meaning are conducted in privacy. In all modes of reading, students should understand that comprehension means they have understood the author's intent and incorporated these meanings into their own thinking.

The only way for teachers to truly know whether readers understand what they have read is to have discussions about the meanings they make. And, should a teacher need to check for decoding and fluency, they can have students read a passage silently first, before reading aloud to the teacher or peers. This gives students the freedom to make approximations and then to re-approximate their attempts for meaning (just as adults do!). This way, any performance can maintain student efficacy.

Choral Read? :)

positively to the intentions behind our learners' approximations honors their abilities to use oral and written language. The same is true as we respond to our young writers' stories. When a child writes a story about a beloved kitty dying, our first response should be as a human being, which involves focusing on the meaning contained in the story on the page. Sometimes, we're tempted to focus on the spacing, spelling, and punctuation or on the paragraphing, topic sentences, and details. When we respond to a message being communicated, we demonstrate respect for and build trust with our learners, increasing engagement. By responding to students' meaning and accepting their approximations, we teach children that their lives and stories are worth writing about, and, most importantly, that they have something to say (Calkins, 1994).

In both talking and writing, there can be no expectation for children to produce fully articulated responses and attempts before we respond to their meaning. In reading, we also can't expect word-perfect reading (i.e., accurate reading, such as on a running record) before we discuss the meanings students are constructing. Students can't spend the majority of their time working on just decoding, with little time devoted to comprehension. In other words, we *can't* wait to work on comprehension until decoding, perfect or otherwise, is achieved.

One last thought about Approximation: As teachers, we recognize and discuss the importance of risk-taking as students attempt new learning. Approximations and our responses to them are central to developing a community of learners who put themselves out there. When we honor students' approximations in an unfamiliar undertaking or an at-the-edge-of-their-understanding task, inquiry and exploration thrive. This inquiry and exploration, in turn, develop our learners' confidence in their own abilities. For our community of learners, confidence eliminates the sense of risk, thereby strengthening engagement. If we want students to learn, how we respond to their approximations is vital and fundamental.

> *If we want students to learn, how we respond to their approximations is vital and fundamental.*

Thinking about Our Own Meaning-Making:

• **In your classroom, how are approximations honored by teachers? By students?**

• **How are approximations used to support learning?**

• **How does honoring approximations affect Engagement?**

Response

Learners must receive responses from exchanges with more-knowledgeable others. Responses must be relevant, appropriate, timely, readily available, and nonthreatening, with no strings attached.

Into the Classroom

It was the middle of a shared reading experience with the group of lively first graders introduced in the previous segment on Approximation. Debra, their teacher, was preparing to introduce the big book, *A Pizza for Bear*, for the first time. (This is the book for which the students would write alternative endings a few days later.) She began by asking the students what they knew about bears. The responses included:

"They eat fish."

"Some bears like to eat honey."

"They make a hole for her babies in the winter."

"They have sharp claws to climb trees."

At this point, Debra placed the new book on the easel. Talk immediately began, as the students spontaneously shared their thinking about the book with their partners, without any prompting by the teacher. After a few moments, Debra brought the group back together and noted their behavior. "You know what I noticed?" Debra said. "You're doing just what readers do when they see the cover of a book and they start reading the title. They start getting excited about the story that they're going to read."

More to the Story
Video of a Shared Reading Lesson Introducing *A Pizza For Bear*

Video of the lesson described above can be viewed at:
https://www.teachingdecisions.com/shared-reading-first-reading-of-squeakys-big-adventure/
The vignette shared above begins at 5:06 in the video.

Teaching Decisions Affecting Response

Teachers spend a lot of time at the beginning of the school year (and continuing throughout the year) teaching students not to blurt out, to always raise a hand to speak, to wait to be called on before speaking, for one person to talk at a time, to listen to the person speaking, and to speak up because they're speaking too quietly—being in control of when and how group interactions proceed in a classroom is a lot of work! The effort requires a great deal of our attention and necessitates a great deal of patience, for all involved. But what if we changed our response? What if we honored the excitement, the engagement, and the *thinking* that reading a compelling text generates? What impact would that have on our practice and on our learners?

In the example of her approach when introducing a new book, Debra recognized and honored the excitement and joy that comes when viewing a book with a cover *that was specifically designed to elicit that excitement and joy*. These kids were doing exactly what the author and illustrator, by deliberately choosing the cover art, wanted readers to do. By responding to the readers' obvious interest in the book

More to the Story
Responding Differently during a Reading Lesson to Ensure Engagement (and All the Other Conditions, Too!)

	Classroom incident	Language and behaviors for compliance	Language and behaviors for Engagement
Before Reading	Teacher shows cover of a book and students get excited. They begin to shout out thinking or talk with neighbors.	"When everyone is sitting nicely, I'll start reading. I'm waiting for everyone to be quiet."	"I can tell you've got thinking going. Talk with your partners." (It is not always necessary to include whole-group sharing after this turn and talk.)
During Reading	At a particularly exciting part or when something happens in the book, a child blurts out something she or he is thinking.	"You need to raise your hand to talk."	Acknowledge the idea with a smile and continue reading. OR Invite the student to say more about that thinking. OR If many students are blurting out their thinking, use a turn and talk with the same acknowledgment in the cell above in "Before Reading."
After Reading	Teacher finishes reading the book and there are lots of comments like: "Oh, I liked that book," and other expressions of excitement.	"What is the main idea of this book?" OR Use a set of comprehension questions or worksheet to complete. OR Always make kids write about the book.	"Turn and talk about what you're thinking now. What did you think about the book?" OR "What was your favorite part? Talk with partners." OR Invite students to talk about their ideas about a part of the book with partners, then invite them to draw and write about those ideas.

and their purposeful need to talk about it, Debra put this need first. Her response gave the students time and space in which to respond in an authentic way. Her comment about their reading behavior helped them recognize themselves as doing "just what readers do," thereby strengthening their engagement in the reading experience. If we label excitement, joy, and thinking as misbehavior, students will soon stop that instinctive or natural behavior, to their detriment and ours.

Additional Thoughts about the Condition of Response

When learning to talk, children are surrounded by caregivers who already know the language(s) the children will ultimately have to control and use. These caregivers regularly respond to a child's utterances. For example, when a child approximates language by asking for "wa-wa," a parent responds, "Oh, you want some water." The language of this response gives the child immediate feedback that the message was communicated and understood. Communication between the learner and the significant other is honest and positive, with no hidden agenda. This no-strings-attached response is very different from a response leaving the child feeling inadequate in what was attempted. With this kind of response, the adult does not expect that the child will immediately reproduce the exact response that was given by the adult, whether in that moment or in exchanges that follow, and communicates this through their words and actions. However, we do expect these immature responses to gradually conform to more conventional language (see "Upping the Ante" on page 100).

As teachers, our responses, sometimes referred to as feedback, also must be honest and positive, related to meaning, and without a hidden agenda. Our language, actions, and attitude must not imply or reveal frustration, annoyance, or disappointment that the learner didn't learn what the teacher "taught." To do so risks undermining the relationships built, which determines the degree to which students engage with our demonstrations. As Debra acknowledges the excitement and thinking the students have when they respond to the cover of their book, her response increases the likelihood of a positive, meaning-making experience as they read together. Especially with novice learners, noticing what *is* working or being attempted, rather than just focusing on what isn't, upholds our relationship with the learners and nourishes an environment built on trust and respect for them. Focusing on what learners are doing that is working has two huge payoffs for teachers.

First, learners may not be aware that what they are doing is working, which means they're unlikely to realize they should keep doing whatever it is. In many instances, if we just focus on something students aren't doing, the students will stop doing what was successful and begin doing the something different that was suggested. Peter H. Johnston (2012) says we might more accurately consider what we say as *feedforward* rather than *feedback*. In Johnston's words, the goal is to "expand the vision of what is possible and how to get there." Noticing and naming what a learner is successful with and perhaps then offering an additional something-else-to-try is a way to use and build on a successful experience to set up expectations for the future.

Second, through our responses, we position learners to offer the same kind of responses to each other. What we notice and name models behaviors and language for students to use as they offer responses to each other. In fact, supporting students to respond to peers is a goal for classrooms designed with the Conditions of Learning

Consistency among grade levels.

in mind. In these classrooms, independent learning times are not expected to be silent. When students talk to each other during reading and writing times, they give and receive responses. ("I like your drawing." "How do you spell Mom?" "I liked the part when the caterpillar ate through all the food.") Conversations focused on what students are doing, such as in a reading conference or a guided reading lesson, provide examples of responsive language and responses that include indications of both the student's intentions and the processes they applied. ("You were trying to figure out that word, weren't you? The way you checked the picture and the first letter of the word helped you know for sure the word was *cat*.") The more we support learners to hear process-oriented responses and the more opportunities we can offer them to give each other such responses, the stronger our community of young learners (and young teachers) becomes. This strengthens engagement as learners become models for each other, and strong engagement deepens their beliefs in their own abilities.

> *More to the Story*
> **Learning Takes Time**
>
> Sometimes, the most challenging part of teaching is realizing that responses from a teacher or another student do not necessarily mean the learner will immediately engage with and internalize those responses. A student's next attempts to forge understanding may (and probably will) also be imperfect. Incorporating new learning takes time, approximation, and practice—and patience, for both the learner and the teacher!

Upping the Ante

There are likely to be times after extended periods of immersions, demonstrations, and responses when we recognize that a child isn't focusing on what we intend. This is a signal the child may need a more explicit and direct response from an adult. Teachers may consider "upping the ante" when we realize learners aren't learning as expected. This is a metaphor for "raising the stakes." Upping the ante should occur, however, only after multiple demonstrations have taken place and ample time has passed.

When a young child is learning to talk, a time may come when a parent decides a more direct response is warranted if the child isn't attending to demonstrations. For example, when a two-year-old child says "wa-wa" for *water*, a parent might respond with a smile and a language demonstration connected to meaning: "Oh, you want some water. Let me get some water for you." But imagine the same child is four or five years old and still saying "wa-wa" for *water*. At some point, a parent may begin directly telling the child to use the more age-appropriate, conventional term.

More to the Story
Upping the Ante and the Process of Application

We include discussion of "upping the ante" here within the Condition of Response. When we ask students to directly try on what was demonstrated, we are actually using the Process of Application. We discuss the Process of Application in Chapter 8.

("Big girls and boys say water, not wa-wa.") The parent may also resist fulfilling the request until the child uses the more age-appropriate language, sending the message to the child that the communication was ineffective. The exact timing of when this more explicit request materializes will vary, often depending on cultural conventions or on information received from one's particular source of support for parenting (e.g., one's mother, mother-in-law, or the latest child development best seller).

More to the Story
Prompting and Coaching Readers to "Up the Ante" While Reading

To "up the ante" for students who rely too heavily on pictures and ignore print, a teacher may decide to use some specific prompting during a small-group lesson or in a conference. After the reader reads a page or two of text, a teacher might prompt the child to check the meaning gained from pictures against the words they see on the page. The teacher might say something like, "What you read makes sense with the pictures. How else can you check to see whether you're right?" For students needing this degree of coaching, truly effective teachers use this prompt on *all* pages read, including those the reader has read correctly; otherwise, the teacher is monitoring for the reader, noting that the student erred just by asking "Are you right?"

If this prompt doesn't generate the checking behavior desired by the teacher, it's important to remind the student that what makes sense (meaning) has to also align with the words on the page (visual) and sound grammatically correct (structure). The teacher might say something like: "You read _____ [repeating the child's reading]. That makes sense and sounds right. Does that work with the letters and words you see?" This type of prompt reinforces that readers must check to see whether what they read looks right with the words they see. The teacher might conclude, following the student checking and, ideally, self-correcting, with something like, "You looked at the pictures. That's very helpful. And it's important to check to see whether what you read looks like the words on the page, too." When teachers use this kind of language to make note of and name the reader's attempts, they reinforce the reading behaviors being approximated.

And, if readers are unable to self-correct, the teacher may then choose to undertake additional word work. This could occur at the end of the lesson, using examples from the book just read. The teacher might also decide to plan additional skill and word work in future lessons. Any such sessions would again involve contextualizing the skills or words under study by using examples selected from the books the students have already read.

Effective teachers make this type of explicit request regularly and systematically. They up the ante on what they expect from students after ample demonstrations and applications. A common classroom example is when readers in the early stage of reading development, using text levels E and F (Fountas and Pinnell, 2017), continue—even after multiple demonstrations—to rely too heavily on the illustrations or photographs in a book. They may ignore the words on the page, in essence creating their own versions of the text, overlooking the author's word choices along with other print information. While reading with perfect accuracy isn't always expected, reading fairly closely to what the text actually says is important in supporting meaning-making. Cross-checking meaning with print information becomes especially important as students read more-challenging texts and nuances are implied through specific word choices. Effective teachers expect students to check their reading among the different systems and to keep the integration of all sources of information—meaning, structure, and visual—front and center.

Deciding when students need a different response, an additional nudge, that moves them from the Conditions of Approximation and Employment to the Process of Application for a particular aspect of learning is challenging. It lies in knowing how to acknowledge approximations and knowing when to use responses that up the ante, as we raise expectations and insist that the learner takes on more individual responsibility. In many cases, any such decision is heavily influenced by the teacher's professional resources. A teacher may seek out more-experienced teachers, for their expertise, or professional books and websites that delineate expectations for various stages of reading development. Determining when to up the ante and expect more from a student can be a challenge for even the most experienced teacher, and applying this approach may require him or her to consult multiple sources. Seeking out these resources promotes and feeds our professional growth as educators. Relying on such resources should always be viewed as an indicator of a teacher's commitment, resourcefulness, and professionalism.

Thinking about Our Own Meaning-Making

- In your classroom, what kind of responses do you provide *for* your learners?

- What kind of responses do you encourage *from* your learners?

- Have you ever had to "up the ante" for a learner?

- How did you do it?

- How do these responses affect Engagement?

Conclusion

The five Conditions of Learning discussed in this chapter—Expectation, Responsibility, Employment, Approximation, and Response—when optimally present, increase the probability of Engagement in the immersions and demonstrations we provide. Intentional use of language and instructional actions by teachers promotes the creation of powerful learning settings, or environments, or ecosystems. The synergy—the interactions and interplay—among the Conditions is discernible to teachers who are aware of and intent on creating the strongest places in which learning can occur.

Within classrooms intentionally implementing the Conditions of Learning, a strong theoretical base about learning is necessary. This provides teachers with a fundamental knowledge for making teaching decisions that support intended learning. Our next chapter adds one more theoretical layer. That layer is language development and use.

Thinking about Our Own Meaning-Making

• **What intentional experiences in your ecosystem of learning "enliven the soils"?**

• **What do you choose to bring into your learning setting because of its inherent value to learning?**

• **What "toxic" behaviors, activities, or language have you stopped doing or using simply because they didn't support a healthy or happy learning culture?**

• **What mismatches exist between your theory of learning and your expectations and responses to learners? How does this affect Engagement?**

• **What mismatches exist in how you support student responsibility, provide opportunities for employment, or use approximations to recognize and honor students' learning? How does this affect Engagement?**

• **What other big ideas are you holding as you reflect on this chapter? What questions do you have?**

"Learning, I propose, is primarily a social
rather than an individual accomplishment."
——Frank Smith, *Joining the Literacy Club: Further Essays into Education*

Chapter 7

Language: The Bridge
between Learning and Teaching

As we said in Chapter 1, many professional books focus on how and what to teach. This book intentionally lingers in theory to help us understand *why* we do what we do in the ways we do. While we intentionally wrote the previous three chapters to highlight instructional practices viewed through the lens of the Conditions of Learning, we pause, in this chapter, to add one more layer of theoretical understanding about learning.

Regardless of how it may sometimes feel, learning doesn't have to be difficult or arduous or troublesome or convoluted. As literacy consultant Lyn Reggett has noted (personal communication between Lyn Reggett and Debra Crouch, 2005): "Reading is complex but it doesn't need to be complicated." As constructivists, we believe Lyn's statement is true for all learning and teaching. But, to teach something complex in an uncomplicated manner requires particular understandings about learning, such as how learners collaboratively construct meanings.

It requires particular understandings about the ensuing teaching, such as the difference between a transmission model and constructivist model of instruction. These understandings provide a basis for distinguishing between these two sets of belief systems, avoiding a mishmash of ideas from both of these varied viewpoints of how learning occurs. Being able to distinguish between these viewpoints allows a teacher to explain and justify the theory that guides their thinking. An indicator that this distinction exists is found when teachers can articulate their theory of learning. This positions teachers to examine and critique the ideas that cross their teaching paths for trustworthiness and credibility.

Throughout this book, in the examples of classroom practice, we have attempted to communicate beliefs about cultures and environments conducive to learning using what nature has already worked out. The models of teaching we propose are designed to make the process of *all* learning as uncomplicated and straightforward as possible for the learners. While learning certainly takes effort and engagement on the part of the learner and inherently involves some productive struggle, teachers should strive to develop learning situations that are as uncomplicated and barrier-free as possible. The Conditions of Learning underlie a vision of classrooms where learning opportunities mirror this belief.

We believe uncomplicated learning and teaching also requires particular understandings about language, its development, and its use. These same cultures and environments that bring the Conditions of Learning to life foster language development and its use alongside literacy, mathematics, and other school learning. In our thinking, language serves as a bridge between learning and teaching.

But, what does it mean to fashion a teaching environment that encourages an uncomplicated and straightforward learning process, one where the Conditions of Learning are fully realized? What specific understandings about the relationship between language development and its use and learning and teaching are necessary to put the Conditions into place to create this learning and teaching culture? And how does our classroom Discourse—the thinking, language, and behaving we use in the classroom—evolve and mature to support and enable a straightforward learning culture based on the Conditions?

Our understandings about the relationships between language, learning, and teaching shape, affect, and change the learning culture we are striving to create in our classrooms. This chapter explores understandings about language, its use, and its development. Without a strong theoretical understanding of constructivist pedagogy and how language develops, an absence of learning may result, without teachers ever understanding why. In these learning cultures, the teacher's role is one of guide, facilitator, and mentor for his or her students. How learners come to view themselves is one outcome of how teachers fulfill this role. What students are capable of achieving is limited only by teachers' expectations of them.

What students are capable of achieving is limited only by teachers' expectations of them.

Learning and the Brain

We broadly describe learning as a process of constructing meaning. Central to all learning is language. In fact, Halliday (1973) equated learning language with *learning how to mean*. Neuroscience has evolved to further support our understandings of how the brain, language, and learning mesh (Hogenboom, 2019). And, as we shared in Chapter 2, changing the mental metaphor is

We broadly describe learning as a process of constructing meaning.

changing how neuroscientists design and interpret their research. By changing their mental construct from one focusing on input and activation of particular regions of the brain to one seeking to understand how our brains process what is experienced, new visions of what is cognitively possible emerge. This has implications for educators and classroom practices.

In what they refer to as "conversational duets," researchers Hirsh-Pasek, Alper, and Golinkoff (2018) emphasize the role of child and adult turn-taking interactions filled with listening and responding. These interactions, they found, increase the connections in language and social regions of a child's brain. Since this learning is based on oral interactions, it implies that discussions are central to how we learn to mean. This distinctly contrasts with models of learning based on telling or transmitting information.

In research led by Rachel R. Romeo (Romeo et al., 2018a, 2018b), a neuroscientist and speech-language pathologist at Boston Children's Hospital, she and her team used brain scans to demonstrate an increase in the connections in the pathways between two major areas of the brain important for language development when children engaged in back-and-forth conversations. The connections between different regions of the brain are what usually give rise to cognitive functions, not the isolated areas (Buzsaki, 2019). Romeo stated (as quoted in Hogenboom, 2019), "We found that more conversation correlated with stronger connections in this pathway, which in turn related to children's language skills." Her team concluded that these connections made through conversation could speed up processing in the language and social areas of the brain. This makes sense in that both those areas underpin human relationships. Learning, we know, is closely tied to our emotional state (Brackett, 2019; Jones and Kahn, 2017; Wolfe and Brandt, 1998). Again, this contrasts with learning settings in which teachers do the majority of the talking and, therefore, the thinking.

The human need to communicate is innate (Jackendoff, 2010; Edelman, 1987; Halliday, 1975, 1978). This necessitates learners simultaneously developing the language necessary for communication as well as the social skills that make such communication possible. In turn, these language skills provide a foundation for further conversation, which leads to higher-level cognition. In other words, the areas of the brain necessary for language and, hence, cognition seem to work together better when learners have the social skills to communicate. These areas simply develop more readily with conversational turns (Romeo et al., 2018a, 2018b). Or, as educator Ralph Peterson (1992) says, "The way we learn has nothing to do with being kept quiet."

Another group of neuroscientists, from Princeton Baby Lab, found that, when children and caregivers engage in interactive play, their brains become "coupled together" (Piazza et al., 2020). According to researchers like Elise Piazza, of the Princeton University Neuroscience Institute, activities such as singing or reading cause brain activation patterns to converge. Her team also noted that, when taking part in separate activities, the "neural synchrony" between learners' brains disappeared. "It's as if you become so tuned in that you're operating not as two people, but as one. That's where we believe the learning gets heightened and takes place, and that's what conversation brings you," Kathy Hirsh-Pasek, who directs the Temple University Infant Language Laboratory in Philadelphia, says of the "neural synchrony" work (as quoted in Hogenboom, 2019). Teachers, peers, and caregivers involved in meaning-based experiences with learners, it seems, are essential to learning. One of those meaning-based experiences, one can infer, is reading and thinking together.

Other brain researchers are changing their mental metaphors, too. Many are rejecting the view of the brain as a computer that processes stimuli in a coding fashion in favor of one of meaning-making with a focus on connections being made. For example, in his recent book, *The Brain From the Inside Out*, neuroscientist Gyorgy Buzsaki (2019) concludes that the brain is not simply absorbing stimuli in a passive fashion and then seeking to represent it through neural code, what he calls an "outside-in" model. Our brains, he contends, are active organs and part of a body that is actively intervening in the world. He calls this an "inside-out" model. Our brains, Buzsaki wrote, have evolved not to just absorb and represent things but to help us survive as we act upon what we perceive. The brain is structured to do just this. This active exploration of the stimuli being encountered leads to meaning-making. As Cobb (2020) writes, "the brain doesn't just represent information: it constructs it."

Learners' brains construct meaning using whatever stimuli, or medium, is available—printed, graphic, oral, etc.—while thinking and interacting alongside other learners. The meanings we make from the stimuli received, and the connections that develop within our brains, are continually adjusted, updated, and revised as we talk and learn more. That's how the active, continually processing brain works. Learning doesn't stop with "the end" or at "goodbye." And, it definitely doesn't happen in isolation or in solitude.

Learning doesn't stop with "the end" or at "goodbye." And, it definitely doesn't happen in isolation or in solitude.

So, while there are educators who equate the complexity of the brain with difficulty in learning, whether that is learning language or learning to read, write, or do math, we agree with neuroscientist Yves Fregnac (2017). He cautions that, by focusing so much on the individual components of brain processing, "all sense of global understanding is in acute danger of getting washed away." By focusing on just the sets of sensory and processing neurons without linking this to the meanings made and the behaviors that result, Cobb (2020) says, "we miss the point of all that processing."

Brain research, we feel, shows us the *potential* for developing our learners' brains through the active, purposeful experiences and language-based, social interactions we put into place on a regular basis. It is these meaning-based interactions between learners and teachers that develop the connections necessary for all learning, whether that learning is about the words we speak, the numbers we add, or the symbols we read.

Thinking about Our Own Meaning-Making

- **How does brain research influence your instructional practice?**

- **How does the research you're reading align with your belief system of learning?**

Language as a Bridge between Learning and Teaching

We endorse Halliday's (1973) theory that learners "learn language, learn through language, and learn about language simultaneously." In Halliday's statement, the key idea is represented by the word *simultaneously*. Halliday is not alone in these beliefs about learning, as we noted in Chapter 2. Other eminent scholars such as James Britton (1970), Frank Smith (1983), Don Holdaway (1979), Douglas Barnes (2008), and Peter Johnston (2012) also share similar views of language development and use.

Language, as we see it, is more than just words being used. It includes any set of symbols used to construct and share meanings. These symbols can be *patterns of sounds*, as in the oral language we learn as children or the whistling languages developed by some communities. Language also includes *patterns of visual symbols*, such as those found in written language, art, and mathematics. Lastly, language is also found in *patterns of movements*, as we observe in dance, sign language, gestures, facial expressions, and mime. Each of these different systems of communicating includes its own set of symbols that are recognized and interpreted by those who "speak" the language. As speakers shape their communication, they make decisions about how to structure that communication on the basis of their message and the relationship they wish to establish or maintain with others.

> *Language, as we see it, is more than just words being used. It includes any set of symbols used to construct and share meanings.*

In the real world, some of these systems are used at the same time, as when we use hand movements, gestures, or facial expressions to accompany the sounds we're uttering. And, while in school learning environments we often see reading, writing, speaking, and listening as separate components of language use, in reality, they function as an interconnected expression of meaning-making.

In Chapter 2, we defined Discourse as a theory that ties the varied relationships and the ways of behaving within a particular setting into a cohesive framework. This theory attempts to explain the ways of thinking and behaving that members of any group expect others to adopt and use when engaged in whatever the group's "business" happens to be. These ways of thinking and behaving include the language they use, which also can reflect the group's relationships, values, and beliefs.

When applied to classrooms, this theory would include ways of thinking and behaving, including how language is used, by both teachers and students. From a teacher standpoint, for instance, it would include how a teacher refers to students, how a teacher organizes space and time, and how the teacher and students respond to one another. For students, it may include recognizing how school "works"—the importance of attending to the teacher's demonstrations, recognizing appropriate times to talk instead of talking at will, and being cooperative in sharing the attention of the teacher with others. Language is the mediator, the bridge, in all these learning and teaching scenarios.

> ### Thinking about Our Own Meaning-Making
> • **How do you define language?**
> • **How does your definition influence your instruction?**

Fostering the Language Bridge between Learning and Teaching

The understandings about language development and use we have outlined above are necessary to put the Conditions of Learning into place in a way that supports the learning and teaching behaviors necessary for a true learning culture. We believe that this layer of pedagogical understanding about language serves as a bridge between learning and teaching—and between the Conditions of Learning and the Processes That Empower Learning. Language is part of discourse and simultaneously plays a role in shaping discourse. Without a deep understanding of language and its role in shaping discourse, the Conditions, and the Processes that arise from their application, tend to become things we do rather than a framework for thinking about learning. This framework shapes how we provide space, time, and resources in a classroom setting.

As we've stated throughout this book, the language of our thoughts, our self-talk, as well as the language we use as we teach, reflects the beliefs we hold and mental metaphors we use. And, these beliefs and metaphors directly sway the instructional opportunities we provide. Our beliefs and metaphors shape the experiences we create for learners to think and behave in certain ways. This is how understanding language at a deep level serves as "a bridge" between learning and teaching, an example of a mental metaphor.

Most teachers, for instance, think and say they value writing and note its importance by using it as the primary means for students to demonstrate comprehension; most high-stakes tests do so as well. But, shouldn't we value using graphical means of demonstrating our comprehension and communicating our thinking just as much? If we value written language over graphical expression, we may not consider drawing as legitimate, or as important as written words, as a way to share one's understanding or communicate one's messages. This may cause us to discount a student who excels at artistic representation of ideas but struggles with composing complete sentences. We may end up negating strengths through the means we use to measure or communicate student understanding (see Chapter 5 for Vivian Gussin Paley's story of Walter).

Another example is when teachers imply independent reading time is a "reward" for a student's "work" being completed (i.e., "When you finish ___, you can read your book."). Through this mental metaphor and the behaviors and understandings it generates, reading for meaning in self-selected books is designated as less important than the other tasks. Reading for enjoyment and learning through meaning-making isn't portrayed or valued in the same way. Rather, it is downgraded to busywork and time filler after you've finished the "real work" of learning. This discourse, including the teacher's language and how it is used, reflects how those who create and maintain such learning settings believe literacy classrooms in particular (and classrooms in general) should function. And this isn't conducive to learning.

A second aspect of the bridging role that language plays in linking learning and teaching is how it supports students to become effective *users* of language. In his ongoing research, Brian studied the ebb and flow of teaching–learning behaviors in classrooms in which teachers were successfully using the Conditions of Learning as a framework to inform teaching. As he coded the data from these classrooms, he began to notice some commonalities developing for the learners where teachers understood that the Conditions functioned in a synergistic relationship. These commonalities centered on how the learners viewed language as a tool for communication. Teachers who were successfully using the Conditions never let a chance go by to communicate the message that literacy was learnable, exciting, interesting, satisfying, and a worthwhile enterprise that could improve students' lives. These teachers continually reinforced the message that all students could "do" this thing called literacy!

The first commonality noted among the learners was the *confidence* they had as users of literacy. As readers and listeners, they were engaged, seeing themselves as capable of making meaning using both written and oral language. As writers and speakers, they were confident about using language to meet a range of needs. This confidence was self-extending, leading them to become even more effective users of language as a means of both *knowing and communicating*.

The second common element found in these classrooms was the students' belief that literacy could help them *achieve a range of personal and social ends*. Students in these classrooms were convinced that literacy makes life "good" (e.g., provides enjoyment, pleasure, information, access to power, equity, justice, and other accoutrements of belonging in our society).

Another commonality among the students was a *commitment* to literacy and the wide range of behaviors it brings. These behaviors include:

- a strong sense of ownership of his or her own meanings;
- a willingness and/or readiness to engage with responses to his or her thinking, whether presented orally or in writing;
- a willingness to take risks when making decisions as he or she shares thinking;
- an awareness of a range of options for making such decisions;
- a willingness to predict and/or reflect on the potential effects his or her thinking might have/did have on others;
- a readiness to accept advice and revise thinking;
- the linguistic and/or rhetorical knowledge necessary to justify his or her linguistic choices in both oral and written language; and
- a willingness to share his or her thinking with members of the community.

Lastly, Brian noted a fourth common element among the learners in classrooms where teachers were successfully using the Conditions. These students were able to articulate (in age-appropriate language), explicitly and soundly, their knowledge, opinions, and beliefs about literacy, its uses, and the range of possibilities for using literacy to further one's own life.

To summarize, the language we use when we think and talk and practice in our classrooms and the understandings about language and its uses that develop for our students link learning and teaching. Understanding language in this way serves as a cognitive bridge, a mental metaphor, between learning and teaching. Understanding these two aspects of language is essential if we are to construct learning opportunities that are both barrier-free and uncomplicated. And, the Conditions can't be fully appreciated or applied without these understandings. Neither can the Processes That Empower Learning.

Commonalities among Learners Who View Language as a Tool for Communication

Confidence—Students see themselves as capable of making meaning using both written and oral language and as effective users of language as a means of both *knowing and communicating.*

Use of language to achieve a range of personal and social ends—Students understand how literacy makes life "good" (e.g., provides enjoyment, pleasure, information, access to power, equity, justice, and other accoutrements of belonging in our society).

Commitment—Students have a commitment to literacy and the wide range of behaviors it brings, such as a strong sense of ownership of their own meanings and a readiness to accept advice and revise thinking.

Ability to articulate (in age-appropriate language) ideas about literacy—Students can share, explicitly and soundly, their knowledge, opinions, and beliefs about literacy, its uses, and the range of possibilities for using literacy to further one's own life.

In the following classroom vignette, we notice language and its use by both students and their teacher. We explore how the teacher's belief system about learning affects the opportunities being provided to the students and the teaching decisions she is making. We also explore how the learning opportunities support the students to engage with literacy. These types of learning experiences are necessary to promote the range of literate behaviors identified by Brian in his research.

Thinking about Our Own Meaning-Making

• **Consider students you've taught who became successful literacy learners and those who didn't. What behaviors or attitudes did these learners have?**

• **How do you think those behaviors or attitudes developed?**

Into the Classroom

The six first graders in the guided reading lesson sat on the floor in a circle with Debra. They were participating in a lesson demonstration Debra was providing for a team of first-grade teachers at the school. This lesson was occurring near the end of the students' first-grade year. After introducing herself and discussing the reason for all the adults watching, Debra gave a copy of the same book to each student and suggested they explore it themselves. The students independently looked through the book *Spiders* (Feely, 2009), unreservedly sharing things they already knew about this topic as prompted by the vivid photographs. Several children strengthened their claims by drawing the group's attention to specific photographic details that linked to their declarations. The discussion moved quickly and enthusiastically.

"They have eight legs. See, I can count them, one, two, three, four . . . ."

"Spiders make webs to catch bugs. I saw a spider web like that at my house."

"Sometimes they're furry—ewww!—and different colors, too."

"Sometimes they're big or really little. Spiders are scary."

At this point, Joseph, who had been nodding along as each of these ideas emerged, added, "They eat insects. Well, they don't really eat them. They suck their blood." The other first graders (along with Debra) were simultaneously horror-struck and amused by this idea, both of which, of course, delighted Joseph.

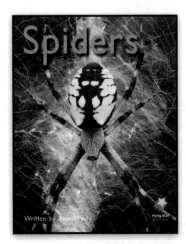

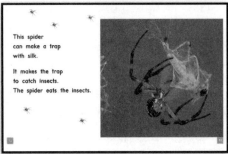

As the lesson moved on, the group returned to the beginning of the book to read, think, and talk more about author's ideas shared on each of the book's pages. A distinctive change seemed to occur in the group's dynamic. For some reason, rather than continuing to share easily and excitedly, the readers now settled for rote recall of factual information read in the book. In other words, the ideas from the book became the focus for their discussion. They rarely linked what they already knew and had shared to what they were learning from the author. Debra believed they were capable of more-complex thinking.

Later in the lesson, after students had read about various ways spiders catch insects to eat, Debra decided to remind Joseph and the other students of an idea shared in the initial discussion.

Debra: *Joseph, you shared earlier you thought that spiders don't actually eat the insect—they just suck the blood. Did you find out about that idea in this book?*

Joseph: *No, it just says they eat the insects.*

Debra: *Hmm . . . why do you think the author didn't include your idea?*

Joseph, after pondering the question for a few seconds, sagely replied, "The author didn't say 'suck the blood' 'cause this book is for little kids. That might be too scary."

Teaching Decisions Related to Language Use and Teacher Expectations

Within any lesson, a teacher's beliefs and understandings about language and its use will impact decision-making. In this lesson, Debra obviously believed that asking Joseph probing questions would offer him the opportunity to make and extend the mental connections necessary for learning to mean. By revisiting his earlier idea, Joseph had the opportunity to think more deeply about a concept of which he has considerable knowledge. Debra's probing questions subtly nudged Joseph to consider how his thinking differed from the ideas in the book and helped him determine possible reasons for this discrepancy. In this way, he was also able to articulate and demonstrate his thinking process for others in the group.

Through this interaction, Debra demonstrated her belief in the student's ability to "go beyond the information given" (Bruner, 1973). Through her theory of the reading process, implicitly communicated by her question, Joseph was nudged to use his background knowledge as a step toward critical understandings about how texts, and reading in general, work. Her expectations of the learner as a capable, critical thinker were also communicated. Debra recognized that, while the text level under discussion may have been thought of as "lower level," Joseph's potential for deeper thinking was anything but.

The vignette also indicates that Joseph, a first grader for whom English is a second language, is "reading like a writer" (Smith, 1987). By this, Smith means that, as well as reading to comprehend the information, Joseph is also attending to the linguistic and content decisions an author has made based on the intended audience for the text he or she plans to create. As Brian found in his research, being able to articulate this idea is important for literacy learning. Through her questions, Debra nudged Joseph to think in these ways.

One long-term outcome of subtly directing readers' attention to these aspects of a text is that it can lead to an understanding of the relationship between the words and phrases an author chooses when composing a text and the intended audience and purposes of that text. The meanings being constructed by Joseph demonstrated a beginning awareness of audience ("little kids") and purpose ("not be too scary"). As Brian found in his research, this understanding supports literacy learners to achieve a range of personal and social ends. All this bodes well for Joseph's future development as an empowered literacy user.

Unfortunately, though, in his educational life, Joseph was already labeled a so-called "struggling reader" and was in the so-called "low group." Formative assessments indicated he, along with his group members, read a text at level D. For most districts that rely on leveling systems (Fountas and Pinnell, 2016a), level D texts are well below what first graders are expected to decode and comprehend at the end of the school year. Hence, the label the "low group."

More importantly than text level, though, is this: What might this label mean for the learning and teaching opportunities Joseph, and others like him, encounter in his school life? What might it mean for the language and, hence, the thinking he experiences? And what might it mean for the language he uses to think about himself as a learner? The expectations we hold and communicate through the experiences we offer determine the responses learners make, and, ultimately, what they learn.

Impact of Language on Learning and Teaching

"The league of learner you are depends significantly on the learner you are expected to be and expect yourself to be" (Perkins, 2009). For students to develop language, literacy, and content, they must be expected to think in ways that connect understandings within these areas. In other words, teachers must cultivate powerful thinking with students regardless of text levels or grade levels or genre. Why? Because our expectations of students link directly to each student's engagement in what is being learned. Engaged learners expect themselves to be capable of learning what is there to be learned, and this expectation directly influences the responsibility they assume for their own learning. Engaged learners see themselves as members of a group of learners, as insiders, as full participants; disengaged learners simply don't.

Using Joseph and his classmates as an example, let's consider how being labeled a "struggling reader" in the "low group" affects the expectations and the language used within the literacy journey for a young learner and others like him. Typically, the instruction for those labeled "struggling" centers mostly on deficits and filling gaps rather than valuing what students bring and providing opportunities to build on the students' approximations. Often, when children find themselves in "low groups," the discussions they encounter are basic. So, too, is the language use and the thinking that results from this use. Instruction, for these learners, centers primarily on the text content or word analysis (both of which are important but not sufficient).

Imagine what happens if a child experiences lessons that are only about the words on the page or what the *author* says. In such cases, what the student brings is ignored because he or she has been prejudged as belonging to the "low group." Will the teacher ask for what students know, finding the gold in what is offered? Will the teacher trust and value learners' approximations and ask probing questions of those learners? Or will the teacher default to telling students information, believing the students won't understand unless they are directly told? How teachers respond to these questions influences the language students encounter and, thus, the thinking that defines literacy and learning for students. How we view a student and the language we use to define him or her *for ourselves* matters because it directly impacts our expectations for the learner, our language use, and the learning that results.

Mary Ellen Vogt (1989, 2000) found that teachers' perceptions of learners affect the kinds of discussions, interactions, and opportunities provided for learners. These teacher perceptions lead to qualitatively different experiences of language and its use for learners perceived and labeled as "lower." Unless we use language in a way that promotes the kind of thinking, feeling, and being we want all students to experience and, ultimately, engage with, the instruction for any student—especially those labeled as "struggling" or "lower level"—is likely to go "awry" (Allington, 2006). The opportunities to make meaningful connections in the brain evaporate. To become successful learners, students must be surrounded by language complete with explanations of how the language, and the thinking it supports, works. This language and these explanations should be embedded within the Discourse of Meaning-Making.

To become successful, students must engage with and employ all aspects of the Discourse—language, behaviors, attitudes, and so on. As Brian's research found, the way the Conditions of Learning are put into place has a powerful impact on how learners come to see their relationship with language and its use. The belief system of the teacher plus the Discourse that arises from that belief system can alter the ways the Conditions of Learning are interpreted. These interpretations can promote or hinder learning. For example, if a teacher believes that mastery of all letters and sounds must occur before students can experience guided reading lessons using texts with rich sentences and ideas, he or she may withhold this kind of instruction. (This thinking signals, "They aren't ready for guided reading yet.") The Discourse will reflect this linear approach to reading instruction, with instruction restricted to single-word-per-page texts or texts based around a single phonic element.

The kind of instruction students receive or don't receive directly impacts the confidence the learners develop, one of Brian's descriptors of effective literacy users. As a consequence, many children who are labeled "low," "struggling," or "intervention" remain as such. This is not due, at all, to their abilities and capabilities but to the limited opportunities to experience and appreciate the benefits and power that literacy brings. Language as a meaning-making tool remains outside their grasp, at least as far as school is concerned.

Thinking about Our Own Meaning-Making

• **In your classroom, what perceptions of your learners have influenced your expectations?**

• **How were those expectations communicated through your language use?**

Making Meaning through Language Use

In his influential collection of essays on literacy learning, *Joining the Literacy Club: Further Essays into Education* (1987), Frank Smith coined the phrase "the literacy club" to describe a culture, or group, of people with particular literate understandings and ways of being. To become a member, one must be apprenticed to existing members. Those in the literacy club, or any club, develop particular patterns of language to express meanings and understandings. Just as those who practice yoga speak of "chakras" and "coming to the front of your mat," those in the literacy club speak of "the best-seller list," "Have you read . . . ?" "I used the index," and "What are you trying to do as a writer?" The language of the literacy club, as for all clubs, is meaningful, useful, and collaborative. It defines the members *as members*. As Smith (1987) noted, "We talk like the people we perceive ourselves to be."

In all learning situations, whether in a yoga class or a kindergarten class, there is a language underlying and influencing what is being learned. Understanding the language (the words as well as any physical demonstrations) being used in any learning setting is necessary for a student to understand what the teacher is saying, asking, demonstrating, etc. Without a thorough understanding of the language being used, the expectations for a learner's success have suddenly become conditional on whether the learner can make sense of what is being asked of him or her in the language the teacher uses.

In all learning situations, whether in a yoga class or a kindergarten class, there is a language underlying and influencing what is being learned.

For example, when a teacher says, "What is the sound the beginning letter makes in this word?" students could be confused by the references to *letter* and *word* and how the word *sound* is used in a specific fashion in this phonics instruction. Some young learners have been known to voice their confusion in some version of this statement: "But letters don't talk." Perhaps using language such as "What sound does this letter *carry*?" could subtly change the metaphor from letters "making" to letters "carrying" sounds. This change of teacher language recognizes that letters don't make sounds, they represent sounds.

Within any group setting, group members must learn to control, or learn, patterns of language to establish a true sense of membership. This results from the immersions and demonstrations they witness. Such patterns of language are peppered with both subject-specific vocabulary (photosynthesis, isotope, etc.) and common words used in specialized ways (such as the word *letter*, which can be both something a postman brings and a written symbol). Controlling, or learning, these patterns of language is essential for membership in a particular learning culture. These patterns and structures of language are central to the range and type of content-specific meanings that members of the group are expected to employ to shape how they both think about *and* communicate this content. For successful and confident literacy learners in a classroom setting, Brian found that having control of language to think and talk about what was being learned was a commonality among the young learners.

How Genre Affects Language Use

Knowledge of genre helps us understand the decisions about language use and structure an author makes to communicate intended messages. In other words, knowledge of genre gives us access to the particular devices, including language use, an author has utilized to communicate ideas. As an aspect of Discourse, each genre has its own specific purpose, overall structure, linguistic features (i.e., word choice or syntactic patterns), and a shared recognition of the genre by those using it (Hoyt, 2018; Gibbons, 2001; Stead, 2001; Derewianka, 1990). Knowing about genre and being consciously aware of these various defining features enables us not only to understand the ideas communicated by others but also to communicate our own messages using the language patterns that the genre demands. These understandings are among the commonalities of the literacy learners in classrooms using the Conditions of Learning successfully.

More to the Story
Genre in Everyday Life

While we often connect genre to school-based literacy studies, the concept exists in the everyday vernacular, too. For instance, when we phone the cable company to complain about our service, we embrace the genre of *complaining*. Our beliefs about how to complain most effectively and to whom so as to get a satisfactory resolution to our problem color how we present the issues. These beliefs heavily affect our Discourse—language, behavior, tone, etc. In everyday vernacular, the purpose of, and audience for, our complaint determines the words, phrases, and intonation we choose. Complaining about one's cable service to an old drinking mate would require quite different linguistic choices than complaining to one's member of Congress!

Smith (1987) introduced the phrase "reading like a writer" to distinguish a kind of reading through which one consciously attends to how a text is constructed, focusing not just on ideas presented but also on what we perceive to be intentional decisions made by an author. This could include a range of author devices. Those choices are indicated by the genre the author has chosen as the means of communication (Mooney, 2004). Each genre offers a different way of communicating our purposes through the language decisions made by authors, including not only their word choices but also the organization of ideas, visuals selected, etc. "Writers of different genres see and think in different ways" (Nichols, 2019b).

In a professional development session that Debra was leading with teachers from grades four to eight, with the goal of crafting a unit on Opinion/Argumentative Writing, Alexandra Rocha, an eighth-grade English Language Arts teacher, reflected on her students' understandings about communicating through writing. "The students produce writing and follow the structures we have taught, but they don't seem to understand the *purpose* of the structures. They don't understand *why* there's an introduction or a thesis statement." This was a powerful observation, the first step in "teaching the writer, not the writing" (Calkins, 1994).

Based on this reflection, Alexandra and her colleagues decided their unit should include extended immersion, leading this group of teachers to identify multiple examples of persuasive and argumentative essays to read, think, and talk about with their students before they asked students to write in the genre. This exploration of texts, they felt, was necessary to support their students in understanding the things writers of these texts do and *why* they do them. They would position their students to read like writers of persuasive and argumentative essays, reading multiple examples of the genre to identify and understand both the content (what the piece is about) and the author's point of view (how he or she frames the topic). Each piece would be further examined to determine exactly how the author constructed the piece to communicate that point of view. Through the reading and writing experiences Alexandra and her colleagues craft for their students, these young writers will be positioned to make those same purposeful decisions for themselves, a hallmark of successful literacy users.

Margaret Meek, in her seminal book, *How Texts Teach What Readers Learn* (1988), wrote, "The most important single lesson that children learn from texts is *the nature and variety of written discourse*, the different ways that language lets a writer tell, and the many and different ways a reader reads." Without this knowledge about texts and the decisions an author makes about language to communicate clearly and effectively, students typically struggle to develop the common elements shared by the effective users of literacy, elements that emerged from Brian's research.

Thinking about Our Own Meaning-Making

• **In your classroom, how does your understanding of genre affect your reading and writing demonstrations?**

• **How do your students use genre to make meaning?**

What Ultimately Becomes Possible?

There is much more than a tenuous link between language and learning. They are inseparable. Members of groups develop knowledge, ways of being, and language patterns—a Discourse—that not only identifies them as group members but also fosters communication and discussion with other members. Each discussion builds language as it strengthens the connections being constructed about what is being learned. When we talk about language in this manner, it becomes central to what is being learned—and what is to be learned is dependent on the language being used. Alongside this, the language we use and opportunities we offer support students to develop beliefs in themselves as learners. Each of these views about the role and purpose of language is inherent in the idea of learning language, through language, and about language simultaneously (Halliday, 1973).

And, as Frank Smith reiterated, it's up to those of us already in the literacy club to take on other learners as apprentices for membership. Like apprentices, literacy learners have varying degrees of competence in the language, skills, strategies, behaviors, attitudes, and knowledge they ultimately will control. The experts who shape and deliver instruction should consider each learner's entry point and adjust their teaching accordingly. Scaffolding for learners based on the assumption of learners with different entry points will significantly challenge a linear, step-by-step, one-size delivery system for all.

In an apprenticeship model of instruction, literacy and language are understood as tools for making meaning. Once we adopt this viewpoint, our instruction begins to change. The Conditions become more prominent in our thinking as we nurture the connected language, literacy, and learning settings, supporting our learners' brains to strengthen the connections necessary for extended growth. Contextualized learning opportunities, such as those described throughout this book, become our norm. When we craft instruction in silos with times designated as exclusively for literacy, or math, or science, or social studies, we may be limiting the possibilities for our learners.

Questions about our practice shift as well, from "How long is a guided reading lesson?" to "How will I use guided reading to support my learners today?" and from "Do I need to read aloud to students every day?" to "How will I use a read aloud approach throughout the day to support my students to think and talk well together?" Questions like "Is it OK to just have independent writing a couple of days a week?" suddenly don't make sense anymore, as our own mental metaphors of what it means to support learners undergo a shift from a rigid view of "doing" instructional approaches to "using" the approaches flexibly.

We craft lessons in different ways, too. Wondering *whether* we will have turn-and-talk times within a lesson changes to wondering *when* we will have turn and talks. Even the way we approach teaching phonics adjusts when we see print as a meaning-making tool. We recognize the need to be explicit as we call out letters, sounds, word parts, and patterns and *also* appreciate the necessity of showing children how these elements help us read and write in meaningful, holistic ways.

Changing Our Focus by Reframing Our Thinking

| Instead of thinking "Am I doing this right?"... | ⮕ | We think, "How does what we are doing support my learners to make meaning?" |

Our often-repeated question from the beginning of the book, "Am I doing this right?" is replaced with "How does what we are doing support my learners to make meaning?" Changing our belief system, and our mental metaphor, leads to changing our thinking, our language, and our practice. And *this* is what leads to student learning.

How We Support Learners Through Language

Learning and teaching opportunity	Examples of instructional language	Effect on the Conditions of Learning
In the guided reading lesson at the beginning of this chapter, Debra asked Joseph to compare his thinking to that presented in the book, rather than having him focus on just what the text said.	Instead of saying: "What did the text say? Was that the same as or different from your idea?" Say: "Why do you think the author didn't include your idea?"	The teacher's response to Joseph's thinking **demonstrates** that the teacher values and expects Joseph's thinking to be his own. This influences Joseph's belief in himself as a learner, fostering **engagement**, and offers him the **responsibility** to share his **approximations** of meaning-making.
In chapter 4, during Trish's read aloud lesson with *The Other Side*, she used a student's question to drive a revisit lesson. Rather than stating Maya's question herself, she asked Maya to restate her question.	Instead of saying: Maya asked a question. She said . . ." Say: "Can you share your question again?"	Because the student takes **responsibility** for sharing her thinking, rather than the teacher repeating the question for students, the student **demonstrates** powerful thinking for classmates. This **response** sets up **expectations** for students to attend to the thinking of others, defining their thinking as important and inspiring student **engagement**.
In Chapter 6, before independent centers time, Debra gave students name cards to indicate the "work" they would like to share with her after their independent reading and writing centers. These name cards were given to students before they began working independently.	Instead of saying: "Today, I will check Trinika's work after centers." Say: "I can't wait to find out what you'll share with me today!"	This **response** to students' anticipated participation (their **employment**) expresses an **expectation** that students are **responsible** learners. This kind of **response** supports the teacher–student relationship, strengthening **engagement**.

Conclusion

As Howard Gardner (2009) reminds us, "the world of the future will demand capacities that until now have been mere options." The language our learners begin to use directly affects the ways they see themselves as learners and the ways they view literacy as a tool for future learning. Through the language we use in our learning settings, we position students as readers, writers, speakers, and listeners—as meaning-makers. Our ability to use language to accomplish this is affected tremendously by our belief systems and mental metaphors about how language and learning occurs and the instructional decisions we make as a result. To create classrooms that promote, support, and maintain deep learning, the role and function of language as a meaning-making tool must be both understood and appreciated at a deep conceptual level. Because, when we understand how language acts as a bridge between learning and teaching, our goals become more holistic, with social, emotional, physical, and cognitive learning integrated throughout our instruction. Our goals become simply to make meaning.

Understanding the role of language and its multifaceted relationship to teaching and learning sets the stage for the Conditions of Learning to strengthen, thereby creating space for Processes That Empower Learning to emerge. In Chapter 8, we examine these Processes more closely, the kinds of processes of learning and teaching that appear when teachers intentionally use the Conditions of Learning as a framework for making instructional decisions. These Processes provide interactions among all the learners that are necessary in classrooms for learning language, through language, and about language simultaneously (Halliday, 1973).

Thinking about Our Own Meaning-Making

- **How do you think your theory of learning and teaching aligns with current brain research on language development and its use?**

- **How have you structured lessons so students "learn language, through language, and about language simultaneously?" What effects do you observe in your learners?**

- **How do you invite children into the "literacy club?"**

- **What is an example of a mismatch between your theory of learning and the instructional language you use or have used? What adjustments to your language would more closely align with your theory of learning?**

"Our work with purposeful talk is constructive.
It's not to regurgitate the known but to construct the unknown."
——Maria Nichols, *"Literacy and Language—Knowing Learners, Knowing Texts,
Knowing Practice"*

Chapter 8

Processes That Empower Learning

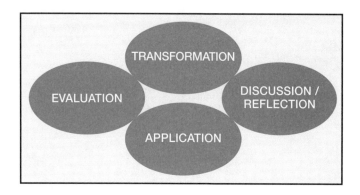

In this chapter, we describe four Processes inherent in classrooms that intentionally focus on bringing the Conditions of Learning to life. In such classrooms, language is seen and understood by all as a meaning-making tool. Literacy and content learning, in these classrooms, is tightly intertwined with the development and use of language.

Whatever "club" we want children to learn their way into, teachers become necessary designers and collaborators with students for what is to be learned.

Frank Smith (1988) said the teacher's role, ultimately, is to ensure that the literacy (or math, science, etc.) club exists, and that every child should be guaranteed membership. Whatever "club" we want children to learn their way into, teachers become necessary designers and collaborators with students for what is to be learned.

So, how will both implicit and explicit teaching occur to guarantee membership in what we will call the *learning club?* How might teachers intentionally craft instruction to support the Conditions of Learning so that language, literacy, and learning intersect and overlap?

After more than four decades of careful recording and analysis of classroom settings, Brian has identified the following four teaching and learning Processes that consistently accompany successful attempts to apply the Conditions of Learning. In these classrooms, teachers intentionally support meaning-making in the learning club. These four Processes are: Transformation, Discussion/Reflection, Application, and Evaluation. Embedding these Processes into the ebb and flow of classroom practice not only increases the depth and durability of the learning but simultaneously honors and encourages approximations as a valid and powerful strategy when learning new ways of knowing and being. Such findings strongly suggest that these Processes are not just about learning to talk or learning literacy or math or science. They also apply to the real worlds of work and play.

More to the Story
Reminder Definitions of Processes from Chapter 3

Transformation—This process enables learners to use and apply constructed meanings in other settings, events, and experiences. Transformation isn't simply copying the person who is demonstrating or memorizing by rote what is being taught; learners actually transform what is learned into something that is uniquely theirs.

Discussion/Reflection—We learn best when we talk with others about our understandings. Talk with others (or, as is the case with reflection, talk with ourselves) about our thinking allows us to construct, clarify, interpret, adjust, and expand our understandings.

Application—Learners need opportunities to apply what they've engaged with; doing so makes it possible for them to approximate what they think they're supposed to be learning and elicit a response from a more knowledgeable other. While the definitions of Employment and Application are very similar, the subtle, but important, difference is in who determines what is being applied or employed.

Evaluation—As we apply, discuss, and transform our learning, each of us evaluates our own performance by asking, "How am I doing?" Building reflection time into our teaching experiences supports this self-evaluation.

What Do We Mean by Transformation?

One can be said to truly *know* and *understand* when one has made that which is to be known and understood one's own. This process of making something one's own requires potential learners to maintain the meanings and/or skills that someone else has demonstrated, even though they might express these meanings somewhat differently. A learner may, for example, use different words to describe what was learned. He or she may apply skills in ways that are just as effective but not identical to those demonstrated by the teacher or coach. A learner may combine ideas from multiple demonstrations to create something unique and individual. We believe this active Process of Transformation is ubiquitous and pervasive in deep learning and understanding, as they work in tandem. Transformation and learning are inextricably connected.

Each learner will develop a unique style, making what was demonstrated his or her own.

Just as no two golfers have exactly the same swing as the one demonstrated by their original coaches, no two pianists play a piece in exactly the same way as another musician. Similarly, no two learners in our classrooms will have the same interpretation of what we demonstrate. While beginners may imitate their first teachers, over time, what was learned changes. Each learner will develop a unique style, making what was demonstrated his or her own. This is what differentiates a constructivist view of learning from the rote-memorization–regurgitation view subconsciously held and encouraged by many educators and parents—and experienced daily by so many students.

More to the Story
Hamilton: An American Musical

Hamilton, which opened on Broadway in August 2015, is one of the most powerful examples of Transformation in American culture today. As many know, the idea for Lin-Manuel Miranda's critically acclaimed Broadway musical began as he read a biography, *Alexander Hamilton* by Ron Chernow, while on vacation. As Miranda started to envision the life of Hamilton as a musical, he was in the beginning throes of a process of Transformation, regenerating and repurposing ideas as he thought about adapting the story from one genre into another. Where he took his thinking became history-making itself: The musical went on to win multiple Tonys, Obies, a Grammy, a Pulitzer Prize, and a Kennedy Center Honors tribute, among many other awards. Miranda and his collaborative team—director Thomas Kail, choreographer Andy Blankenbuehler, and musical director Alex Lacamoire—were deemed "'trailblazing creators of a transformative work that defies category,' a distinction never before awarded by the Kennedy Center" (Aviles, 2018).

Imagine if Miranda's thinking and response to his reading were limited to writing a five-paragraph essay or answering text-dependent questions or filling in a reading log about the biography he read. Or if he'd had someone say to him, "That's not what we're doing right now." We must ask ourselves: Do we limit the potential of our students' responses, and the possibility of Transformation? Or do we create space and use language that promotes opportunities to be a trailblazer?

Into the Classroom to Explore the Process of Transformation

Because Transformation is a significant measure of learning, we offer multiple examples to illustrate this concept.

Reading

While reading the book *The Summer My Father Was Ten* (Brisson, 1998) with a class of fifth graders, Debra encountered powerful thinking from the students, many of whom were learning English as a second language. In this beautiful picture book, a child relates the tradition of planting a garden with her father. And, as they plant the garden every year, she again hears the story of Mr. Bellavista, a neighbor with a "strange" accent—and of an incident that occurred the summer her father was ten. During this eventful summer, her father and his friends destroy Mr. Bellavista's garden in a moment of youthful carelessness. Eventually, after a period of guilt and a heartfelt apology from the father, he and Mr. Bellavista reconcile as they plant a garden together and form a lifelong, life-altering relationship. This story is a powerful reminder of how relationships and traditions can arise from an unfortunate incident.

The students had the same two goals for each of two different read aloud lessons, held over two consecutive days. One goal was linked to reading, the other to listening and speaking. As readers, they were noticing changes in characters over time, and understanding what might have caused each of the characters to change during the course of the story. Their listening and speaking goals involved noticing how the thinking of other students was influencing their ideas.

During the second-day revisit of the text to extend thinking and discussion, a student named Francisco shared an idea with the class that had been percolating over the two read aloud sessions. He drew the attention of his classmates to an illustration late in the book showing three of the book's characters sitting at a dining table after a meal: Mr. Bellavista, the father's mother, and the titular father of the story (as a young boy). Illustrations of Mr. Bellavista earlier in the book show him in drab-colored buttoned-to-the-neck shirts; in this illustration, however, he wears a bright green sweater and is shown laughing along with the father (as a young boy) and his mother. Francisco excitedly noted how the illustrator had clothed Mr. Bellavista in a green sweater, and he shared his theory of the illustration.

Francisco: *I know why his sweater is green. It's like the illustrator wanted us to know Mr. Bellavista has grown.*

Debra: *Can you say more about that idea?*

Francisco: *Well, you know how when Angie said Mr. Bellavista didn't talk to other people and that he was probably lonely and that he wore his shirts buttoned all the way up to his neck, and then James said they were growing the garden together on that other page . . . well, those ideas made me notice that Mr. Bellavista looks so happy with the family on that page where they're in the kitchen. He's not lonely anymore cause now he's in the family, and I noticed his shirt is green and gardens are green and they grow . . . . so, it's like Mr. Bellavista has grown. That's why his sweater is green like a garden.*

Debra: (trying to remain neutral, rather than exuberantly praising Francisco): *Thank you for sharing that thinking, Francisco.*

Readers bring their own interpretations to a text. They gather ideas expressed by the author and/or illustrator, combining them with their own knowledge and the thinking of other learners. Doing so results in a personal amalgam of analysis and synthesis. While we may all hear or read the same words, maybe even see the same illustrations, the meanings we make from any of those elements are our own. In this read aloud experience, Francisco demonstrated his ability not only to notice what appeared in the book but also to use the thinking of others to help him develop a theory about how messages can be communicated within a text. As responsive teachers, we explore ideas a student offers—even when we might not be sure where the student is going or where the idea comes from.

This instructional give-and-take offers both implicit and explicit moments for teachers to lift up the thinking of students. We not only notice the ideas being generated but also help students notice how they arrived at understandings (if they're not as articulate as Francisco about their process!). As Halliday (1973) states, this simultaneous focus on content and process supports students as they develop and learn language to express their thinking and learn through language as they share their own thoughts and hear others share theirs. Students also learn about language as they consider how a genre (in this case, a picture book) communicates meaning in multiple ways. As brain research shows, this give-and-take within discussion is what supports the brain to grow, strengthen connections, and construct meanings (Cobb, 2020; Buzsaki, 2019; Romeo et al., 2018a, 2018b).

Writing

Katie Wood Ray (1999) says that writers write in individual ways, but these ways are not unique. In other words, all writers draw from the same repertoire of techniques; they just apply them differently. For example, one writer might use

Mismatch between Theory and Practice
Preparation and Improvisation

Many times, teachers feel uncomfortable with the seemingly improvisational nature of responsive teaching. Some teachers refuse to spend class time on discussions, because of the unpredictable nature of what might occur, the tangents students might go off on, or the time it will take when there is so much to "cover." Other teachers feel that, to be responsive to their students, they should not *plan* a lesson; they should instead just let the lesson unfold "naturally."

The very thing that supports a teacher to be more responsive may feel like a contradiction: being well planned. And part of that planning involves *planning to be responsive.*

Patricia Ryan Madson's book *Improv Wisdom* (2005) has a challenging subtitle for an educator: ~~Don't Prepare, Just Show Up.~~ But, as one reads her book, the admonition "Don't prepare" is clearly not the same as being *unprepared*. In fact, Madson shares tips on preparing (aka *planning*) that allows for responsiveness—planning to be open; planning to attend to what a partner says; planning to say, "Yes, and . . ." rather than "Yes, but . . ."; planning to accept responses from partners and build from them. All this planning allows one to "just show up."

In teaching, this attitude of just showing up to be responsive is reflected in our planning; what we say yes to is significant.

• Planning to have read alouds with discussion is a yes; planning to tell kids what meanings they must make to ensure they get it is not a yes.

• When a student says something different from your thinking, saying "That idea is intriguing and needs to be explored" is another yes; responding, "We aren't talking about that" is not a yes.

• Knowing your text well is a definite yes; winging it with a teacher's guide is not a yes.

The choices we make are our own, and "we all assume 100 percent responsibility for the outcome of our teaching," which is only "possible when knowledgeable professionals become responsible decision makers" (Howard, 2012).

repetition to draw attention to an idea, whereas another writer might choose to use a different technique. Yet a third writer might use repetition for a completely different purpose. These uses are not unique, just individual to the writers.

And where do these writers develop this repertoire of techniques? What any writer knows as a writer, he or she knew first as a reader. In this way, books serve as artifacts in demonstrations of good writing. When teachers use books, or mentor texts, they provide both implicit and explicit demonstrations of what a writer does to craft a text. Genre, and the language signifying that particular genre, can become a strong layer within these demonstrations (see Alexandra Rocha and her colleagues in Chapter 7, page 120.

In these instances, when a reader is making meaning of a text, that reader is free to change words and phrases used by authors *as long as* intended meanings are maintained. When writing, the notion of transforming what has been demonstrated into something fresh and different requires a learner to take control of or assume ownership of the text's concepts and relationships (i.e., the language of the text). Through "reading like a writer," the writer comes to understand the author's devices and decisions related to a particular genre. Writers then can draw on these understandings to meet their own writing needs.

In Trish Candia's kindergarten class, poetry was a popular genre. The class had deemed Shel Silverstein a favorite poet after multiple read aloud sessions; the students frequently read teacher-made charts of favorite poems by him and other poets during shared reading sessions. In a writing unit on poetry, Trish used the poems in *Kids' Poems: Teaching Kindergartners to Love Writing Poetry* (Routman, 2000) to immerse her students in examples of the kinds of poems they might write for themselves. She also demonstrated one technique for writing a poem that used words, phrases, and sentences from a personal narrative she had previously written. During independent writing time, the students revisited their own writing, and each tried to craft a poem using the technique Trish had modeled. Jorge, one of Trish's students, focused on a story he'd written about basketball, with the intent of transforming it into a poem. He circled words and sentences within his narrative to use in his poem: Basketball, basketball (circled twice), basketball is fun, I like basketball.

One of the ideas about the genre of poetry that had been discussed throughout the unit was about "line breaks": how poets consider the words that go together on each line, and how a line break makes a reader pause before moving on to the next line. To determine the effect of a line break in their poems, the students read their poems aloud to a partner. Together, they deliberated on how the poem sounded when words were joined on a line or when a line break was used intentionally to make a reader pause.

When Trish conferred with Jorge, she read his words aloud and asked him if he'd like the first two words, *Basketball* and *basketball* to appear on the same line or on consecutive lines. She read the words quickly together, as if they were on the same line. And then she read the words with a pause between them, as if they were on consecutive lines of the poem. Jorge thought for a moment and said, "I want them on the same line." Trish then asked, "Why do you want them on the same line?" This brilliant five-year-old poet said, "Because when they're on the same line, you say them fast and they sound like a basketball when you dribble it."

Jorge reflected on his story and how basketball is meaningful for him as he crafted his poem. He made decisions about word choices that all poets make. He considered line breaks as a tool for communicating meaning. These decisions suggest a growing understanding of the genre. Furthermore, he is able to explain coherently his transformation process, meaning that he is more likely to transfer the learning to other contexts. Finally, Jorge demonstrates a burgeoning understanding of relationships that exist among different forms of writing. One could say he is being launched as a writer!

Each of these decisions positions Jorge as a confident user of language, exhibiting the same commonalities as the students in Brian's research. Jorge was able to see the effect of his writing as he transformed the demonstration he had observed his teacher give into his own unique piece of poetry. The joy he felt (and his teacher felt) with his decisions, and his ability to articulate the purposes behind his decisions, are key in helping Jorge to become a lifelong literacy user.

Integrated Learning Wholes

It was centers time one spring day in Debra's kindergarten class. As she was jotting notes about a just-concluded guided reading group, Justin and Heath popped up alongside the table. Bouncing on their toes with excitement, they requested breathlessly, "Ms. Crouch, can we make a graph of kids who have signs on them and kids who don't have signs on them?" Trying to catch up with the thread of their thinking, and hear more clearly what they were asking and she might be agreeing to, Debra said, "That sounds interesting. Tell me more about your idea."

Justin said, "Well, you know the book we read [he shows the cover of a text his group read in guided reading the week before] and on the last page it said 'Signs on T-shirts, Signs on me.' Me and Heath could make a graph of kids in the class who have signs on them, on their T-shirts, and kids that don't."

Debra smiled and agreed this would be a great idea. "Do you need any help from me?" she asked.

Justin thought for a moment and said, "We need you to draw the line for us." They were basically saying, *use the ruler to draw a straight line separating the columns in our graph.*

The boys scurried off to the writing center to get the necessary clipboard, paper, pencils, and trusty ruler, bringing these items to Debra to assist in preparing the graph. After she drew "the line" and initiated a discussion on what the heading for each column should be, the boys were off to collect their "data." (Epilogue: This became a two-day project because they "didn't get everybody today," and they wanted to be thorough. Presenting the results from their graph became a math lesson a few days later.)

Throughout the school year, these boys had been engaged in many learning experiences that contributed to this transformative thinking. In math sessions, they'd learned that graphs can be a powerful tool for moving from concrete to representational to abstract thinking about numbers. They'd regularly used this tool for counting, comparing, and understanding concepts such as less than, more than, and equals. In literacy sessions, they'd been encouraged to write multiple story extensions from well-known and loved books. They'd used these story adaptations and ideas to generate personal stories, indicating that they were getting the idea of how to "read like a writer" and apply what they'd learned from such reading to their own writing (Smith, 1985).

For these learners on this day, it was as if two separate circles of what had been learned in literacy and math sessions had subtly overlapped. Just as in a Venn diagram, where two separate sets of meanings exist but share overlapping ideas, each boy's thinking combined to create a new "whole." This act of combining what were once separate meanings into new wholes is the core of Transformation. Experiences such as these, coupled with the encouragement to explore their own thinking, supported Justin, Heath, and the other learners to construct ideas in unique ways. The flexibility to pursue personal projects and interests, not just those of the teacher, is necessary for students to make learning their own.

Justin and Heath demonstrated the commonalities of learners in classrooms where the Conditions of Learning are applied in a constructivist way. As we think about these users of language and literacy, literacy makes classroom life "good." The strong sense of ownership of meanings being made was obvious. These students were willing to engage with others about their ideas and make the decisions necessary to achieve their literacy goals. Preparing for the task itself demonstrated an awareness of options open to them, a readiness to accept advice from the teacher as they debated column headings, and the ability to justify their own linguistic choices. Days later, as they shared their graph with their community of fellow learners, they listened to suggestions and comments as they interpreted their findings from their data. Each of these stances as a learner indicates growth in cognition and the transformative power of thinking for one's self. Throughout this transformative process, the connections in their brains were strengthened through interactions with others (Hirsh-Pasek, Alper, and Golinkoff, 2018; Romeo et al., 2018a, 2018b).

Intentional teaching supports learners to transform what they learn from one setting into something new. What happens for a learner isn't just applying or replicating what was demonstrated. As the learner engages, he or she is required to go "beyond the information given" (Bruner, 1973) to apply, use, and extend the information in a different way. When demonstrations make explicit the decisions

being made, learners are more likely to be able to transform what was demonstrated. So, when Francisco offers a unique interpretation of a text, or Jorge crafts a poem with intentional line breaks, or Justin and Heath share their graph with their classmates, possibilities for transformation become visible. Such teaching and learning encounters truly "alter the trajectory" for our learners (Howard, 2012). As David N. Perkins (2009) reminds us, "The whole point of education is to prepare people with skills and knowledge and understanding for use elsewhere, often *very* elsewhere."

Thinking about Our Own Meaning-Making

• **What examples of the Process of Transformation have occurred in your classroom?**

• **What, in your learning setting, supported this transformation?**

What Do We Mean by Discussion/Reflection?

The Process of Transformation is enormously enhanced through Discussion/Reflection, meaning that a social dimension to learning is mandatory if learning is to occur. Talk with others (or, as is the case with Reflection, talk with ourselves) about our thinking is crucial for us to construct, clarify, interpret, adjust, and expand our understandings. This talk is qualitatively different from the kind of talk that occurs in most classrooms. Collaborative talk of this nature, what educator Maria Nichols deems "purposeful talk" (2019a), supports participants to strategize, innovate, problem-solve, construct, deconstruct, and reconstruct understandings. These discussions honor the constructive intent of the group members. As we said in Chapter 7, brain research shows that interactions are crucial to develop connections in the brain (Cobb, 2020; Buzsaki, 2019; Romeo et al., 2018a, 2018b). This is what the phrase "grow your brain" actually means.

In her most recent book, *Building Bigger Ideas: A Process for Teaching Purposeful Talk* (2019a), Nichols says talk is purposeful when it honors constructive intent,

Mismatch between Theory and Practice
When Classroom Talk Doesn't Lead to Learning

In many classrooms, unfortunately, students tend to be talked *to* and *at*, rather than *with*. This is a hallmark of a classroom using a transmission model of teaching, where teachers believe that information is transferred from the teacher to the student.

Typically, in a transmission model, "good teaching," as defined by some, follows a protocol or structure identified by a teacher's guide. This is often to make the learning "teacher-proof" (Scherer, 2012). We believe it's impossible to "script" talk sessions, however, and discussions dictated by lesson plans often resemble interrogations, with students answering teacher questions, not discussing their ideas.

Even in classrooms where student dialogue is said to be valued, teacher-directed structures and protocols may become dominant to ensure students talk at certain times and in particular ways. In these setups, discussions may be assessed in a meaningless quantitative fashion (i.e., How often did a particular student talk? Did they use the talk starter/stem that was provided?) rather than a qualitative meaning-based manner (i.e., How did a student's thinking change as a result of the conversation? How did a student's thinking change the thinking of others?).

harnesses the power of varied perspectives, and engages participants over expanded time and space. These dynamic processes of "learning, thinking, knowing, and understanding are significantly enhanced when one is provided with opportunities for 'talking one's way to meaning,' both with others and with oneself" (Cambourne, 1995). Purposeful discussion harnesses the power of varied perspectives as a tool for broadening thinking. In classrooms alive with the Process of Discussion/Reflection, learners discover the constructive potential of collaborating with others. This kind of discussion occurs over expanded time and space. Within any such discussion, learners develop the abilities to stay with compelling topics over time, to continue to seek out various perspectives, and to revise previous thinking. This recursive discussing–thinking–rediscussing–rethinking cycle supports "talking one's way to meaning."

Into the Classroom to Explore the Process of Discussion/Reflection

In *Building Bigger Ideas: A Process for Teaching Purposeful Talk* (2019a), Maria Nichols shares a story of a group of fourth graders discussing the book *Dave the Potter: Artist, Poet, Slave* (Hill, 2010). This lyrical picture book relates the life of Dave Drake, an enslaved artisan, who lived in South Carolina in the 1800s. Dave was a prolific and gifted potter who spent his entire life as a slave. He skillfully created clay pots, some of which have survived and are found in museums today. He inscribed his poetry in the clay. As we join this lesson, the illustrations and sparse text have generated a conversation that Nichols describes as a "passionate mix of awe and ire." At one point, the conversation slows, and Nichols, the fourth graders' teacher (i.e., Maria), notices and acknowledges frustration on the students' faces. She begins to explore the source of their thinking.

Maria: *Jaylen, what's going on over there? You're shaking your head.*

Jaylen: *Well—I don't get—the words are weird. Why did he put them* [the poems] *on it?*

Ellie: *On the pots?*

Multiple voices: *Yeah…I don't get why…me, too…*

Nichols realizes the students are stuck, but, rather than adding her thinking to the mix, she honors the approximations of tentative thinking by asking the students to turn and talk with partners. She listens in on several partnerships, noticing the partners' questions and tentative theories; some ask to revisit specific pages; others try to make sense of Dave's poems. Still others wonder about Dave's motives for writing the poems. Nichols listens in and finds an intriguing possibility in a thought being explored by Emilio and Kiley. They are struggling with a passage from the text: "But to Dave, it was a pot large enough to store a season's grain harvest, to put up salted meat, to hold memories."

Back in the whole-group conversation, as Emilio explains his and Kiley's confusion, another student, Cole, joins the conversation.

Cole: *We didn't get that, too—when it said he put in the meat and the memories.*

Kiley: *We—yeah, we still don't get about the meat. But I said, the memories, I said it's, like, poems—it's the memories. It's why he did it.*

Mayesha: *I don't get—the poems—do you mean the poems—that's the memories?*

Kiley: *Well, yeah. It's his memories. Maybe to remember his family—so he doesn't forget because he can't see them.*

Mayesha: (looking quizzically at Kiley, starts to speak, stops, "takes an audible breath as she formulates her words"): *But he—he doesn't tell about them* [his family].

Maria: (looking around the circle): *What do you all think?*

Francisco: *Oh yeah—it could make him remember, you know, when he thinks so he can write the poems, he remembers and maybe it feels good to him.*

After some quiet time with the students clearly processing this idea (evident from their "furrowed brows and pursed lips") and combining this new thinking with what they have read in the book and other ideas they've heard from classmates, one more student, Shawn, "draws from a line on the last page to exuberantly propose a counter theory."

Shawn: But—no, I think—it said "us" . . . to let *us* know!

The students were clearly affected by this idea, exclaiming "Ohhhh!" and "What?" as they worked to reflect and incorporate this new theory into their thinking. They reread the last page of text: "But before the jar completely hardened, Dave picked up a stick and wrote to let us know that he was here." This prompted a chorus of voices. Maria encouraged them to turn and talk once more as they worked to deepen the meanings they were constructing through this discussion.

In this classroom example of Discussion/Reflection, all the Conditions of Learning and the Processes That Empower Learning are present. The students clearly demonstrate the power of talking their way to meaning. They undoubtedly use collaborative discussions with the intent of constructing, clarifying, adjusting, and expanding their own thinking. There is no search for "right answers," only a search for understanding. The various perspectives highlighted in this classroom example both implicitly and explicitly demonstrate the social dimension of learning for these students. The level of engagement is high; these students see themselves as learners capable of figuring out a confusion that arose when reading a complex text. They assume responsibility for their own learning by staying with this topic and being willing to incorporate others' thinking into their own. They're comfortable in moments of silence when they or their classmates need time and space to process; thinking, their own and that of others, is expected and valued. This is what is known as a dialogic classroom, a place where teachers engage students in processes for learning about talk and through talk simultaneously (Wegerif, 2013).

> *There is no search for "right answers," only a search for understanding.*

In her dialogic classroom, Nichols creates a space for Conditions to strengthen. She honors the extended time and space necessary for developing multiple theories about a text; this intentional slowing down of processing when exploring a text provides space for tentative thinking to emerge and big ideas to evolve, supporting the Condition of Responsibility. This kind of Immersion and Demonstration sets students up to be successful in meaning-making. Discussion/Reflection, for Nichols, unmistakably doesn't arise from a litany of questions she asks to get students thinking about certain ideas she believes are important in the book at hand. She trusts her learners to make important meanings for themselves, a key factor in Engagement.

While supporting the Conditions of Learning and the Processes, the Discourse in this classroom also encourages students to learn in ways embodied in a meaning-

> ### *Mismatch between Theory and Practice*
> ### Questions to Guide Discussions
>
> Teachers plan questions to prompt student discussions, hoping that the perfectly written, just-right question will accomplish two big things for them: elicit what students understand and generate strong student discussion. Children, however, are clever. They learn early on that, if they just wait, the teacher will ask a brilliant question—one that is carefully crafted to be open-ended, higher-level, and text-dependent—and that question will provide an inkling of what the teacher is hoping to hear. These thoughtful, strategically written questions are often loaded with information, using academic vocabulary from the text we want students to master. Once we ask that perfect question, students expertly convert the question into an answer and hand it back to us as evidence of their thinking. For many students, even those we deem successful, this is how school works. And, unfortunately, our questions don't lead to engagement with the content and the spirited discussions we crave.

making setting. This classroom example illustrates the importance of a deliberate coupling of the teaching of literacy (or any content, for that matter) with the intentional teaching of talk behaviors. As Nichols illuminates, the ability to engage in discussions, and the accompanying language development inherent in this work, can't be left to chance; it requires multiple demonstrations, from both the teacher and other students. In the demonstrations, students benefit from explicit explorations of language that support productive interactions with others. The willingness to grapple with uncertainty and recognize the same efforts in others is indicative of the kind of teaching that leads to lifelong learning and literacy use.

These students also profit socially and emotionally by attending to more than oral language as they intentionally notice gestures, facial expressions, and body language in addition to words spoken. By being immersed in this Discourse, meaning-making becomes second nature. Through intentional teaching of authentic discussion, thinking, and purposes, the learning setting is enhanced and consolidated. In this classroom, students experience the range of possibilities for using literacy to further one's own life.

Thinking about Our Own Meaning-Making

• How do you support the Process of Discussion/Reflection in your classroom?

• How have you adjusted your instruction to include more opportunities for discussion and reflection?

What Do We Mean by Application?

There is a multilayered relationship between Transformation, Discussion/Reflection, and Application. When people collaborate, they are compelled to interact and discuss the topic or problem at hand. As a consequence of these discussions, we are privy to what others do, say, and think about the topic or problem. Trying on ideas, shaping and reshaping our thinking, deciding what we think now that we've heard others' ways of looking at things—this is how we transform our own ideas and learning. How does this collaboration relate to the Process of Application? And, how is Application different from the Condition of Employment?

There is much inherent overlap between the Condition of Employment and the Process of Application. Both obviously have students making approximations with what was demonstrated. Our expectations are clear as students engage with what we have taught. The difference between the Condition of Employment and the Process of Application has to do with who chooses the focus for the practice.

In the Condition of Employment, learners choose what to attend to, integrate, and practice based on what they personally need for their own learning. For example, kids who are learning to invent spellings are focusing on stretching out words, but the particular letter/sound formations on which they spend their efforts are determined by the children themselves. So, even if the teacher emphasized particular letters, sounds, or patterns in a demonstration, each child chooses what he or she can do and needs to do at that moment in time based on his or her intention—what he or she is trying to communicate as a writer or speaker.

In the Process of Application, there is more emphasis on learners trying out specific parts of what the teacher intended in his or her demonstrations. This is a variation of the Condition of Employment. What sets Application apart from Employment is that the teacher makes the decision on what is attended to, rather than the learner (see the section from Chapter 3 on "upping the ante"). Application involves more of a "what they need to learn or apply" stance.

For a parallel, real-world example, consider the apprenticeship construct: The expert often decided what specific skills the apprentice should apply and when. For example, tailors could decide that their apprentices needed to apply the skill of sewing on buttons, so they would have the apprentices sew buttons on the suits that the expert tailor had almost finished.

As a classroom example, consider that, during a guided reading lesson with earliest emergent readers, learners might be expected to track the print by finger-pointing to each word, because the teacher, having demonstrated this in shared reading multiple times, is asking students to apply what she's taught. But, while the teacher decides *what* is being applied, it's through the collaboration with others that learners get responses enabling them to adjust their approximations.

Into the Classroom to Explore the Process of Application

In many classrooms, practice of what is learned may occur at a particular time of day or in a particular activity: independent practice, independent reading or writing, centers time, work stations. We frame these times as opportunities for children to try on what it is we've taught. In many classrooms, students are encouraged to work alone, to be quiet, because the teacher uses these times to meet with small groups or for conferring, both of which require being able to focus on the individual, or individuals, at hand. For the Process of Application, however, students need to collaborate in order to receive the kinds of responses, necessary for learning to occur as they are applying what the teacher has deemed important.

Independent Reading

"One child, one book, quietly reading" does not meet the criteria for the Process of Application; nor does "one writer, quietly writing." The *aloneness* that characterizes these activities in these quiet classrooms does not allow for the Process of Discussion/Reflection that engages and encourages most learners and leads to Transformation. Nor does being quiet allow the Condition of Employment and Process of Application to be appropriately realized. As we stated earlier, there is a multilayered interaction among Transformation, Discussion/Reflection, and Application.

During independent reading in a classroom with the Condition of Employment and the Process of Application layered in, learners read a variety of texts, both of their own choice and those introduced by the teacher. They read fiction, nonfiction, online content, or illustrated texts, and they bring ideas in these texts together to explore those ideas that have captured their curiosity. They may read in a variety of modes—alone, with partners, in discussion groups—and may read the same or different texts with those partners or groups. However and whatever they read, they are consciously aware that, at some point (or points) in the day, they will purposefully interact with other readers. Discussions of what was read in independent reading should happen regularly. Some of those discussions will be initiated by students and some by teachers. Living a readerly life is the epitome of Immersion and is the strongest expression of Engagement.

Choosing what, how, and with whom one thinks and reads is the most meaningful responsibility a reader can have. Accessible classroom libraries to support this kind of responsible learning are organized more similarly to bookstores than traditional libraries—by topics, genres, and authors. Because students are selecting reading material based on interest, not reading level, teachers help students figure out how to determine *for themselves* whether they understand a text (as is discussed later in Evaluation). This comparative thinking requires students to know what making sense of a text feels like in their brains so they can know when they *don't* understand. Assessing one's own understanding involves ongoing discussions with other readers.

Responding to Independent Reading

Many times, independent time involves a response to a text, often a written response of some sort. The intent of responding to texts is to think and feel more deeply about the text. Again, for the Process of Application to fully support learning, we must broaden our thinking and the demonstrations we provide on what responses to text encompass. Responding to texts should be an opportunity for students to look further into a text to refine initial understandings. They may increase their awareness of how authors use words, language, text organization, and features, and other writerly techniques. Accordingly, they think even more critically about the meanings they have constructed and may also extend discussions with other readers (New Zealand Ministry of Education, 1997). Authenticity in response is essential for engagement to occur in independent reading. If students are required to write about everything they read, they soon disengage with the acts of both reading and writing.

Teachers who understand the true purpose of responding to texts offer students choices for demonstrating thoughts and understandings through a variety of responses—written, artistic, dramatic, graphic—and through calls to action and analysis of our world (to name a few). By modeling a variety of responses to texts, teachers provide students options for how they can go beyond the information given, which allows for Transformation. By providing choices in responding to texts, teachers encourage students to develop responsibility for their own thinking. And, because all texts don't warrant this level of introspection, supporting students to consider whether they respond to a text at all must also be an option. While writing as response to a text is one possibility, it can't be the only one if we want to support Transformation through Application and Discussion/Reflection.

Responses during Group Time

But, to truly support the Condition of Employment and the Process of Application, the most effective teachers think well beyond what we call *independent practice*. These teachers embrace the notion articulated by Peter H. Johnston in *Opening Minds: Using Language to Change Lives* (2012): "Thinking well together leads to thinking well alone." In this view of learning, the thinking work reflects a depth of understanding by students that occurs over time when facilitated by a thoughtful teacher. During our whole- and small-group times, teachers offer frames for "thinking well" about texts, about ourselves as meaning-makers, and about others as fellow meaning-making collaborators. Discussions about the ways texts influence how readers think and feel support authentic immersion and demonstrations. These discussions are essential parts of whole-class lessons that support engagement during independent reading. The examples we have shared of read aloud throughout this chapter, and other lessons from the preceding chapters, are examples of this kind of teaching.

Well-facilitated read aloud or guided reading lessons that occur over multiple days provide models for thinking well. Over time, something important begins to happen: Children themselves come to use the full discourse available in the learning setting. The metaphors we make, the oral expressions we use, the behaviors and actions we demonstrate—all these provide powerful models for learners to emulate in their own thinking. These models are often implicit; the most effective teachers, however, know the power of making them conscious and explicit. For example, in Chapter 4, Trish closed her read aloud lesson in this way:

> As readers, we have been thinking about why characters change in stories. Maya noticed a change in Clover's mama's thinking. She wondered why Clover's mama had changed her thinking about Clover and Annie's friendship. Maya's question helped us think more about why a character in the story changed. Thinking about characters—how they think and feel and how they change in stories—helps us understand stories even more.

This kind of conclusion to lessons, this "process-oriented feedback" (Johnston, 2012), supports students not only to know the powerful thinking they have been engaging in but also to understand how this thinking occurred. This kind of response strengthens each student's ability to think, interact, and apply knowledge and skills successfully in other situations, an ability that characterizes Transformation. And, through highlighting the power of collaboration in their process of meaning-making, students are positioned to see collaboration as a tool for learning that ultimately strengthens the Condition of Employment and the Processes of Application and Transformation.

Thinking about Our Own Meaning-Making

• **How do you include opportunities for both Application and Employment throughout your instructional day?**

Mismatch between Theory and Practice
Learners Who Struggle Automatically Get More Time with an Adult

One of the biggest misconceptions in learning is that a student who struggles needs more time with an adult. It seems counterintuitive to consider the idea of the student perhaps needing something else. Our default in classrooms when a learner struggles is for the teacher (or another adult, or sometimes multiple adults) to provide more demonstrations. And it may well be the case that the learner needs additional examples of what is to be learned. There are, however, other Conditions of Learning that may require more support if learners are to be successful.

- Has the learner had sufficient immersion to understand how what is being learned works within a *whole?*
  - Could the learner, in fact, benefit from hearing more books read aloud to him or her?
  - Might the learner benefit from having a teacher write down his or her story to reread?
  - Might the learner benefit from talking with other students about what is to be learned?
- Perhaps our language and practice has been inconsistent to support strong engagement?
- Or maybe our expectations of a student's ability have been measured and conditional?
- Could providing consistent occasions for a struggling learner to take responsibility and approximate during independent reading or writing have a positive result?

Often, students who struggle to orchestrate all they are learning about meaning-making while reading are the ones who get the least amount of independent time. The decisions we make matter. Deciding to demonstrate shouldn't always be, and *isn't*, our only option.

What Do We Mean by Evaluation?

A continuous thread running through the teaching and learning experiences in this book is the Process of Evaluation. While the terms *assessment* and *evaluation* are familiar and common in classrooms and schools, our take on the Process of Evaluation (with a capital E) goes beyond the typical terminology assigned to those terms. The Process of Evaluation we are exploring here is driven not by our judgments about a learner but by the learner personally. The Process of Evaluation is about self-evaluation, not teacher evaluation.

Potential learners are constantly evaluating their own performances as they engage, discuss, transform, and apply what is being learned, whether it is ironing a shirt, practicing a yoga pose, swinging a golf club, or making the latest iteration of a dish from a favorite cooking show. Learners gauge their own abilities and successes by comparing their approximations of what was to be learned to the immersions and demonstrations of whatever version of the *whole* was presented. (This is another reason why experiencing learning *wholes* is so important.)

More to the Story
What is the Difference between Assessment and Evaluation?

Assessment is often confused with evaluation, and, while they are interdependent, they are different things. *Assessment* is the gathering of data using a particular tool, such as an oral reading record or a rubric. Assessment may also include observational data or some type of scoring setup. *Evaluation* is what we do with the data produced by our assessment. Evaluation involves making a value judgment from our assessment data. The better our assessment, the better our potential evaluation.

For teachers to truly assess and evaluate a learner's understandings and support the student's self-reflections, evaluations of transformed understandings are our best and most accurate measures of learning, not having the student simply reflect back what we taught. Just as with purposeful talk, our goal is not to have students regurgitate the known but to construct the unknown (Nichols, 2019b).

In the early stages of this evaluative process, the closer a learner's attempts appear to be to the models they've experienced, the more successful the learner perceives himself or herself to be. This Process is best supported in an environment that is neither judgmental nor competitive in nature. This accepting environment also supports the transformation process, where learners ultimately take ownership. Within this inclusive environment, learners feel confident and secure to ask themselves, "How am I doing?"

Teachers and peers provide responses to support self-evaluation when they respond to learners' attempts. As discussed earlier in the section on Response in Chapter 6, the relationships in a community of learners are crucial in terms of students engaging with these responses, whether the teacher is an adult or a peer. Existing in a responsive loop, the quality of the responses, in turn, fuel the learner–teacher relationship by supporting the student to continue to engage with demonstrations. In other words, if the response is positive, relevant, and meaningful, learners continue to engage with our demonstrations. However, when the response is negative, irrelevant, and meaningless, student engagement becomes superficial. So do any subsequent meanings being made.

Into the Classroom to Explore the Process of Evaluation

In our opinion, effective classrooms should include opportunities for learners to engage in continuous cycles of *apply–discuss–transform–evaluate*. Throughout this cycle, teachers will participate in ongoing discussions with learners, integrating these discussions into both whole- and small-group opportunities. For example, reading conferences with individual students will provide opportunities to offer responses, giving us a snapshot of each learner and his or her abilities to choose, read, and think about those chosen books. Teachers will construct numerous classroom experiences in which students can hear from the teacher and peers about their own processes for understanding. Those experiences include debriefs at the end of independent reading time or closures at the end of other lessons. Opportunities such as these strengthen students' abilities to become more reflective.

Responses to Texts As a Means to Self-Evaluate

Earlier in this chapter, we discussed the idea of supporting students to use a variety of responses to what is being learned. Each type of response—written, artistic, dramatic, or graphic, together with calls to action and analysis of our world—requires teachers and students to consider how to gauge understandings by students. One technique many teachers use asks students to determine the criteria for evaluating their responses. (The students are often more demanding than the adults!) Through this inquiry approach, students are positioned to be reflective. First, they must consider what is to be learned; then they consider what it means to have learned. Both of these reflections influence students' abilities to determine a change in their own learning.

Teacher Modeling for Self-Evaluation

Throughout this book, we have shared classroom stories of teachers who assume a reflective stance, about both student learning and their own learning. These teachers are more likely to succeed at supporting students to become reflective. A reflective approach serves us well in both assessing and evaluating our own teaching capabilities and supporting our learners to develop the ability to evaluate their own learning. It also models a reflective stance for our learners.

Trish Candia, the kindergarten teacher we met in Chapter 4 in read aloud lessons using *The Other Side*, is a learner herself, as exemplified in the coaching session she had with Debra. She's not afraid to say when she's unsure of next steps in her own practice. This reflective stance permeates her classroom; children seem to sense when they are being taught by a fellow learner. Trish trusts her students to learn what she wants them to learn (and what she recognizes *they* want to learn as well), and she illuminates this throughout the discussions and interactions about texts she has with students. The relationships in her classroom community provide a safe space for her students' initial wonderings about texts and the expanded thinking that occurs as they revisit texts regularly. Discovering what was missed in previous reads is regarded as compelling thinking in this classroom. These whole-group lessons position students to be meaning-makers on their own; they can

Mismatch between Theory and Practice

How Our Belief Systems and Our Assessment Practices Complicate Language and Literacy Learning

Sometimes, our assessments can be narrow in focus, zooming in on item knowledge (e.g., using a capital letter correctly). These types of assessments may use one or two test questions to label a student as deficient in an area such as *sequencing*. In these instances, an assessment might lead us to focus our instruction too heavily on discrete parts of literacy.

Mismatches in the area of assessment can also arise from how data are reported. Many assessments used to ascertain students' literacy understandings categorize students into two or three groupings: yes/no, pass/fail, or red/yellow/green. Literacy learning is often expressed as a literal measure, a "got it/don't got it" valuation of students' abilities. Assessment data using these gauges categorize rather than describe learners.

In both of these mismatches, assessment drives instruction that isn't supporting students to be strategic, to use what *is* effective in their repertoire. They may even be encouraged, implicitly or unintentionally, to stop doing what is working well.

Meaningful assessments should help us understand two important things. First, they help us determine what a learner does and uses when processing within text. Second, they offer us next steps in how to support the learner's processing *overall*, not just his or her isolated skill development. To use assessments in this way requires a teacher to collect, interpret, and reflect on information from multiple sources.

evaluate their individual thinking ("How am I doing?") by recognizing the kind of thinking they are capable of when they construct meanings with their peers. They know, emotionally and intellectually, what it means to make meaning.

In Chapter 5, Jeralyn, a highly reflective educator, reinforced and nourished the same behaviors in her students. In the science lesson where the students were working to make a bulb light, the students routinely illustrated in their science notebooks *both* successful and unsuccessful attempts. Through these disparate recordings, they were able to evaluate their own learning. More importantly, they were situated not only to consider why they were successful but also to ponder why they were *unsuccessful*. This means they were primed to transform the learning from this encounter to other situations. When learners address other problems, they bring two kinds of "know-how" from a focus on both successful and unsuccessful approximations. They can generalize from the knowledge of what does work as well as what *doesn't* in terms of the content. Furthermore, their understanding of the learning process is deepened and extended as they become better problem solvers overall.

In Chapter 6, Debra's use of name cards as a way to touch base with students during centers provides an assessment and evaluation opportunity and also a chance for students to engage in self-reflection. Because the students were identifying *for themselves* what to share as evidence of their "work," making choices of what they felt effectively represented their "best" put them squarely into reflective mode. They had to ask themselves, "What represents *me* as a learner?"

This is what we mean by Evaluation.

Thinking about Our Own Meaning-Making

• **How do you include the Process of Evaluation throughout your instructional day?**

• **How do you support students' self-evaluation through your responses to their approximations?**

Conclusion

Our intent as teachers is to include both implicit and explicit teaching that guarantees membership in the "learning club." Our intentionally crafted instruction and careful use of teacher language and facilitation supports the Conditions of Learning and the Processes That Empower Learning. Taken together, the Conditions of Learning and the Processes That Empower Learning provide a lens for shaping settings that truly nurture student learning. To translate the Conditions and Processes into practice requires a thoughtful teacher who is constantly evaluating his or her own practice and who intentionally considers how to strengthen learning for all students in the classroom. Our final chapter includes templates designed to support every teacher to do just that—analyze classroom practices using the Conditions and the Processes.

Thinking about Our Own Meaning-Making

- How do you intentionally support meaning-making so students are invited into the "learning club?"

- Which Processes that Empower Learning do you support in your classroom?

- How do they align with your theory of learning?

- What mismatches exist between your theory of learning and the intentional language and facilitation you use to support learners?

- What other big ideas are you holding as you reflect on this chapter?

- What questions do you have?

"People try to do all sorts of clever and difficult things to improve life instead of doing the simplest, easiest thing—refusing to participate in activities that make life bad."
——Leo Tolstoy, *Path of Life*

Chapter 9

Using This Theory of Learning to Guide Your Own Practice

To paraphrase the futurist Alvin Toffler, it helps everything go well when we keep the big things in mind so all of the little things go in the right direction. This is what using a theory of learning to shape instruction is all about—using a vision of what is possible to guide the day-to-day decisions we make.

This chapter is designed to support educators engaging in learning opportunities that characterize the professional stance we support. The templates we present are designed as reflective lenses, a means for exploring instructional practice. They offer us the opportunity to shift our questions from external evaluation (i.e., "Am I doing this right?") to a self-evaluative stance (i.e., "How do *I* think I'm doing?").

Making Decisions

In some schools or districts, teachers may feel they have little power to make decisions that affect what occurs in their classrooms. Schools and districts often emphasize time and structures, as these modes are the easiest to implement and measure. However, even within discussions of time and structure, a teacher establishes the tone and

> *This is what using a theory of learning to shape instruction is all about— using a vision of what is possible to guide the day-to-day decisions we make.*

language within a learning community. These ideas are not mutually exclusive. How a teacher talks with students in ways that express respect and kindness, or how a teacher provides opportunities across a lesson for students to talk together to construct and extend thinking, is crucial. These interactions subtly determine the effectiveness of any lesson structure and the ways that teachers distribute and allocate time. Community, content, and classroom organization work in harmony.

Effective teachers continuously reflect on outcomes for learners and the alternatives for achieving them, and they make in-the-moment and long-term decisions based on these reflections. For professionals, the ability to articulate those reflections and the ensuing decisions is paramount. When a decision is called into question, a concern is expressed, or a query is made, effective educators approach the exchange as interested inquiry rather than interrogation. Our goals should be to explain our ideas rather than defend them, to clarify our thinking rather than protect it, to expound on and illuminate our professional decision-making rather than simply comply with someone else's value system. A well-articulated belief system enables and bolsters the ability to assume this stance.

Our goals should be to explain our ideas rather than defend them, to clarify our thinking rather than protect it, to expound on and illuminate our professional decision-making

As we've said before, why we do what we do in the way we do matters to our learners. An articulated belief system, our "why," helps keep the big picture of learning in mind and influences us in the decisions we ultimately make. It also helps us understand more deeply and become more articulate as we justify decisions about our practices, to ourselves and to others.

In Chapter 2, we described a belief system—or perspective, or philosophy—as a synonym for a theory. Our belief system, or theory, and embedded conceptual metaphors about learning guide us in shaping the learning environments for our students. They empower us to be critical consumers of materials and practices regardless of the messenger. They give us support to think through questions that arise for anyone who has ever worked with children. Going back to our opening question—"Am I doing this right?"—our belief system provides the guidance we need to think through "answers" for ourselves.

Changing Practice

Throughout this book, we've called out specific mismatches between belief systems and classroom practices. Each of these mismatches grew from specific decisions a teacher made. Mismatches don't mean we are bad teachers. They simply mean we, or those we've learned from, may not have considered potential or unintended consequences of the choices made for our learners (we all have those experiences, regardless of how long we've taught!). Or, perhaps, our theoretical understandings and instructional practices haven't aligned yet. New ideas, regardless of our initial enthusiasm, take time and energy to implement.

Ultimately, though, we have to acknowledge that, if learning isn't occurring as we intend for our students, it is rarely because our students aren't built for complex learning or because their home lives aren't structured in particular ways. Our belief is that, if learning isn't occurring, it's because our *learning settings* aren't built and structured for such complex learning. On the other hand, if learning continues for our students, it's because we design settings that affirm kids are "made for learning."

As we stated earlier in this book, educators often layer long-held ways of thinking onto new practices, even when those new practices evolved from a very different belief system. Sometimes, we end up with learning environments filled with activities that make our students' literacy lives "bad" (as Tolstoy said) or meaningless or toxic. Such activities essentially consume the time needed for the literacy work we know begets readers and writers—readers and writers who not only can read and write but also choose to do so.

... if learning continues for our students, it's because we design settings that affirm kids are "made for learning."

What Makes Changing Our Beliefs and Practices So Difficult?

It's so easy to fall into repetitive patterns of behaviors in our teaching practices. And, sometimes, that's a good thing; those patterns can make classrooms powerful and effective. One such pattern is a literacy block with consistently recurring organizational structures. For example, teachers just beginning to implement read aloud might use a particular time each day for this practice, whereas more seasoned practitioners might use the read aloud approach across their day (such as in science or social studies lessons as well as in language arts). But, while the structure is repetitive, the learning that occurs within it is not. Repetitive structures like these evoke a sense of normalcy and routine from which to construct the unknown— that's the powerful component. What makes the repetitive structures effective, however, is how what occurs within them evolves over time based on student needs and abilities.

Another powerful pattern can be a centers-based, or stations-based, or Daily 5 (Boushey and Moser, 2006) type of structure within independent time for students. Again, the repetitive nature of the structure for independent time provides a safe and predictable space for coming to new learning. However, it's not the center or station or Daily 5 literacy tasks that change. Structures such as these evolve with the learners. As students become increasingly adept at reading and writing more sophisticated and complex texts, the consistency and predictability of these structures provides time and space for growth and extended learning.

But patterns can also be our downfall when making changes. When we are stressed or lack confidence or are being led down one more mandated path we struggle to value, it's easy to fall back into old patterns of behavior. A read aloud certainly takes less time when we don't use turn and talks for student discussion.

Having students always raise a hand and wait to be called on before they speak is sometimes easier to manage. Organizing our classroom libraries by levels is a much quicker way to get "just right" books into the hands of learners (or so we tell ourselves). But these old patterns can keep us rooted in unsuccessful instruction, producing unsuccessful students.

Practices That Support Change

Implementing structures and processes we know will make a difference for our students is key when it comes to making our practices less confusing and more meaningful. The daily experiences such as read aloud (or shared reading, independent reading, or writing workshop) should reflect the Conditions of Learning in action. As we noted earlier, literacy consultant Lyn Reggett said (personal communication between Lyn Reggett and Debra Crouch, 2005): "Reading is complex but it doesn't need to be complicated." While instruction might seem a complex mix of processes and ways of behaving, it's not complicated. Unless we choose to make it so.

Intentionally supporting effective instruction can start in simple ways. For example, ensuring a read aloud with discussion occurs daily is important. Inviting students to gather for this read aloud instead of sitting at their desks changes the entire lesson. Putting sticky notes into a read aloud text reminds us when to have students turn and talk. These are simple changes that can make a world of difference for students' meaning-making.

Another intentional change is noticing your instructional language. Try out some of the phrasings you've seen in this book or in others. Support yourself by putting a sticky note with the new language into a book at a spot where you think it would be effective. When Trish Candia, who is referenced in Chapter 4, was practicing using more invitational language during lessons, she wrote herself a note reminding herself to say, "Let's all look at ___ while he's speaking." (This was instead of using directional language: "Look at the speaker.") Using notes and other reminders supports you to explore fresh ways to communicate. These are necessary until new language becomes second nature in our instruction. So, as psychologists suggest, instead of trying to stop doing something, we should *start* doing something else (Shortsleeve, 2018).

Bigger changes may require more support. As we said in Chapter 2, we are all bombarded with the latest, greatest teaching ideas, whether these come from favorite websites, through conferences, or from other professional learning settings. As you engage with the ideas being presented, intentionally ask how these ideas will affect your learners and your learning setting. Here are some questions to ask yourself about such professional ideas:

- How does what I'm hearing affect the Conditions of Learning?

- Does it encourage true engagement or is it based on compliance?

- Does it offer students space to approximate and take responsibility for decisions leading to meaning-making?

- Do the demonstrations I'm being encouraged to provide build on the students' experience of wholes so what is being taught is meaningful?

Practices that support change are not just about young learners. They are also true for adults. Our own professional learning opportunities should be based on the same Conditions of Learning outlined for students. This requires us to become our own advocate as we seek out reputable sources of knowledge, practice, and theory. We must be able to distinguish between trustworthy and dubious sources. We must constantly remind ourselves that, just because the ideas expressed are new and flashy—whether online or in hard copy, created by other teachers or by a well-funded company, or labeled research-based or scientific—this doesn't make the ideas effective or important.

In his research session at the International Literacy Association 2019 Conference, P. David Pearson encouraged us to advance our own practices by building our thinking "on your evidence, not on the back of a strawperson" (2019). As we change our own thinking and practice, let's surround ourselves with fellow educators who offer thoughtful ideas that truly support meaning-making and inspire us to make important decisions for our learners.

Using the Conditions of Learning to Make Instructional Decisions

The Conditions of Learning is a well-thought-out theory. It offers a lens, or framework, for examining our existing belief system about learning and the practices we use in our classrooms. It challenges us to think differently as we create the learning spaces we call classrooms and the learning interactions we call teaching. It asks us to be intentional about our linguistic choices and sensitive to the worthwhileness of those who inhabit our learning settings. When teachers have a deep, substantive knowledge of the Conditions of Learning and the Processes discussed throughout this book, they just teach differently. And their students think and use literacy differently as a result.

Using the Templates

The appendix that follows this chapter offers templates for using the Conditions of Learning to examine one's belief systems and instructional practices. As articulated in Chapter 3, the synergistic nature of the Conditions and Processes means they function holistically. While we might, for our own practical purposes, choose to discuss a Condition individually, the synergistic reality of the Conditions means the others are woven throughout our discussions as well. This lack of boundaries between each Condition and Process is inherent in classrooms in which learners are encouraged to use reading, writing, speaking, and listening to explore and make sense of their world.

There are two approaches to using the Conditions of Learning as a lens for examining a learning setting. One way is to capture a teaching and learning event, analyze how what occurs strengthens or weakens the learning opportunities for students, and consider how to strengthen the Conditions and Processes to increase learning potential. Templates 1–4 are structured for this kind of analysis. Template 4 is blank, to use for your own reflection.

In Templates 1–3, we offer further reflection on some of the lessons detailed throughout the book. In the chapters about individual Conditions and Processes, we included a lesson transcript to highlight the particular Condition or Process under discussion. However, because the Conditions and Processes are synergistic, we need to always remember that our instructional decisions affect each Condition and Process *simultaneously*. These templates enable us to tell the rest of the story.

A second way to use the Conditions of Learning to analyze teaching is to focus on an instructional area, such as writing, science, spelling, or math. This provides an opportunity to identify how the Conditions may be applied to the classroom teaching behaviors used to teach the content. Templates 5 and 6 are structured for this type of analysis. Template 5 explores writing through the lens of the Conditions, while Template 6 is blank for your own reflection.

To use these templates, we suggest videotaping a lesson or having a trusted colleague take detailed notes of you and your students engaging in learning. It is essential to capture the actions in the lesson and the language of the exchanges between and among the students and teacher. We also suggest being a colleague's trusted partner–observer. Thinking about teaching without having to "do" the teaching is a powerful opportunity to further your own expertise.

But, just as there isn't a *right* answer for the way the Conditions and Processes influence or guide instruction, the point of these exercises isn't to figure out the right way to do a lesson or activity. Instead, the goal is to strengthen the learning setting by bringing intentionality to decisions that make learning more likely to occur—in other words, to apply intentionality to strengthen the Conditions of Learning and Processes That Empower Learning. We hope these ideas will awaken your own inner decision maker—one of the true signs of a learner.

Appendix

Templates for Exploring Practice through the Conditions of Learning

Teaching Decisions Examined through the Conditions of Learning #1 Read Aloud from Chapter 4, Immersion and Demonstration

Teaching Decisions Examined through the Conditions of Learning #2 Guided Reading from Chapter 7, Language: The Bridge between Learning and Teaching

Teaching Decisions Examined through the Conditions of Learning #3 Read Aloud from Chapter 8, Processes That Empower Learning

Teaching Decisions Examined through the Conditions of Learning #4 (Blank Template A)

Teaching Decisions Examined through the Conditions of Learning #5 Some Suggestions for Turning a Theory of Learning into Instruction

Teaching Decisions Examined through the Conditions of Learning #6 (Blank Template B)

Full-size templates with writable cells for templates #4 and #6 can be downloaded from the website, https://www.rcowen.com/conditionsoflearning.htm

Teaching Decisions Examined through the Conditions of Learning
#1 Read Aloud from Chapter 4, Immersion and Demonstration

Text: The First Revisit to *The Other Side* (Woodson, 2001)
Teacher: *Trish Candia*

Lesson	Teaching Decisions	How the Conditions and Processes are Affected by these Teaching Decisions (Specific Conditions and Processes are in bold)
Ashley: *She said I couldn't swing 'cause I wasn't big enough and I said yes, I was, but she still wouldn't let me play.* Trish: *How did you feel when the girl wouldn't let you play?* Ashley: *I felt sad. I almost cried but I didn't.* Trish: *So, Ashley, you felt sad when someone said you couldn't play. How do you think Annie feels when Sandra says no, you can't jump rope with us?* Ashley: *Annie feels sad.*	Trish probes the learner to support the student to expand her own thinking. Trish helps Ashley relate her connection to a character in the book and understand how this connection helped her understand the character.	When teachers follow up by asking students to expand on their thinking, students make **attempts** free from the fear of being wrong, a critical factor for **engagement**. The teacher has communicated her **expectations** and beliefs that the learner is capable, helping the student assume **responsibility** for her own thinking. These interactions allow teachers to assess authentically and to provide appropriate **responses** to learners.
Trish (to the entire class): *When Ashley remembered how sad she felt when someone wouldn't let her play, Ashley knew how Annie felt when Sandra told Annie she couldn't play* (Refers back to relevant pages in the book) *Connections can help us understand how characters are feeling in a story. They make the story more interesting to us and make us want to know more about our characters. Thank you, Ashley, for helping us understand how our connections help us understand the stories we read.*	Trish helps other students understand how connections help us as readers, using Ashley's connection as an example.	**Response** to students about a process they used supports them to understand how they made meaning (assumed **responsibility**) and why doing so is important for readers (a factor for **engagement**). This articulation of student **employment** of a reading strategy communicates that students have taken **responsibility** for learning and have met **expectations** we have for them as learners. **Engagement** increases as readers see themselves as capable and have a clear understanding of how our **demonstrations** relate to meaning-making.

Lesson	Teaching Decisions	How the Conditions and Processes are Affected by these Teaching Decisions (Specific Conditions and Processes are in bold)
Trish continues to read. A few pages later, Trish read: *"Some mornings my mama watched us. I waited for her to tell me to get down from that fence before I break my neck or something. But she never did."* *"'I see you made a new friend,' she said one morning."* Trish paused, and silence hung in the air. After a few seconds of quiet, Maya spoke up: *I wonder why her mama changed her mind?* Trish was silent, allowing time and space for the other students to respond to Maya's "wondering." No one did. Trish hesitated, then continued reading to the end of the story.	Trish pauses and allows space for thinking to occur. She does not require students to raise their hands to share thinking. Trish's silence gave space for the other students to decide for themselves if they wanted to respond to Maya's question; they did not. Trish also did not offer an "answer" herself.	A belief in learner's thinking and their abilities supports **engagement**. It strengthens the relationship that is crucial for engagement to occur. Offering to students the opportunity to decide when and how to share thinking also supports **engagement**, ensuring students see themselves as "doers" of reading. Not providing easy answers to student's questions sets up **expectations** of learners that they can be solvers of their own questions and problems. This kind of response to a learner increases **engagement** and **responsibility**.

What decisions might you make next time? How will this affect each of the Conditions?

Supporting students to discuss another student's question will strengthen the Condition of Responsibility by turning the discussion over to the students. It can also strengthen Engagement and the Process of Evaluation as the students engage in further discussion about Maya's question. This will make a strong "next lesson" focus.

Teaching Decisions Examined through the Conditions of Learning

#2 Guided Reading from Chapter 7, Language: The Bridge between Learning and Teaching

Text: First Reading of *Spiders* (Feely, 2009) Teacher: *Debra Crouch*		
Lesson	**Teaching Decisions**	**How the Conditions and Processes are Affected by these Teaching Decisions** (Specific Conditions and Processes are in bold)
The students independently looked through the book *Spiders* (Feely, 2009), unreservedly sharing things they already knew about this topic as prompted by the vivid photographs. Several children strengthened their claims by drawing the group's attention to specific photographic details that linked to their declarations. The discussion moved quickly and enthusiastically. *They have eight legs. See, I can count them, one, two, three, four …* *Spiders make webs to catch bugs. I saw a spider web like that at my house.* *Sometimes they're furry— ewww!— and different colors, too.* *Sometimes they're big or really little. Spiders are scary.* At this point, Joseph, who had been nodding along as each of these ideas emerged, added, *They eat insects. Well, they don't really eat them. They suck their blood.* The other first graders were appropriately horror-struck and amused by this idea, which delighted Joseph.	Debra asked the students to introduce the book to themselves rather than having them follow her page by page through the book. She was quiet while the students shared ideas, neither confirming nor denying the validity of their ideas. She laughed along with the children, including Joseph, at the "horror" of his idea.	When teachers support learners to take **responsibility** for their own learning, they nurture the students' belief in themselves as learners. This supports student **engagement**. By accepting all their ideas as equally valid, Debra encourages **approximation** and communicates an **expectation** of them as capable learners. By engaging with the group's meaning-making (the group's "horror" at Joseph's idea), Debra's **response** expresses her acceptance of all ideas. This encourages students to participate without judgment or harm, a key factor in **engagement**. This also supports the Process of **Evaluation**, through which students determine how they're doing with the meaning-making being constructed.
As the lesson moved on, the group returned to the beginning of the book to read, think, and talk more about author's ideas shared on each of the book's		

Lesson	Teaching Decisions	How the Conditions and Processes are Affected by these Teaching Decisions (Specific Conditions and Processes are in bold)
pages. A distinctive change seemed to occur in the group's dynamic. For some reason, rather than continuing to share easily and excitedly, the readers now settled for rote recall of factual information read in the book. In other words, the ideas from the book became the focus for their discussion. They rarely link what they already knew and had shared to what they were learning from the author. Debra believed they were capable of more complex thinking.	Debra attended to the change in the group's discussion and confidence.	Recognizing the unspoken lack of confidence about their abilities to make sense of a text is important for **responses** to the learners. As the children shared, Debra continued to accept all **approximations** from the learners. Her observations about how their thinking changed influenced subsequent **demonstrations** for the class.
Later in the lesson, after students read about various ways spiders catch insects to eat, Debra decided to remind Joseph and the other students of an idea shared in the initial discussion. Debra: *Joseph, you shared earlier you thought that spiders don't actually eat the insect, they just suck the blood. Did you find out about that idea in this book?* Joseph: *No, it just says they eat the insects.* Debra: *Hmm ... why do you think the author didn't include your idea?* Joseph, after pondering the question for a few seconds, sagely replied, *The author didn't say 'suck the blood' 'cause this book is for little kids. That might be too scary.*	Debra recalled Joseph's idea about spiders from the earlier discussion and brought the idea back for deeper consideration. She phrased her question to elevate Joseph's idea to those in the book: *Did you find out about that idea in this book?* She probed to offer Joseph the opportunity to consider why the author had made a decision about how the book was written.	Lifting up a student's ideas in this way validates their **approximations** and encourages **responsibility** for thinking. Phrasing her question in a way that elevates the students' thinking to that of the book's author communicates a belief in the learner to make sense of a topic and text. This kind of **response** to a learner increases **engagement** and **responsibility**. **Engagement** increases as readers see themselves as capable.

What decisions might you make next time? How will this affect each of the Conditions?

Read aloud and shared reading lessons should emphasize that the ideas found in a text are not the "right" answers or the only ideas to value. Shared and independent writing will also be important for thinking about topics from varying perspectives.

Demonstrations in both reading and writing will support engagement for learners. Thinking critically about what is not included in a book will be an important focus while reading and writing texts. This will help students form their own expectations of and beliefs in themselves as capable of making sense of a text. This will also help students recognize that just because a text differs from their thinking doesn't invalidate that thinking.

Teaching Decisions Examined through the Conditions of Learning
#3 Read Aloud from Chapter 8, Processes That Empower Learning

Text: First Reading of *Dave the Potter: Artist, Poet, Slave* (Hill, 2010)
Teacher: *Maria Nichols*

Lesson	Teaching Decisions	How the Conditions and Processes are Affected by these Teaching Decisions (Specific Conditions and Processes are in bold)
At one point, the conversation slows and Maria, their teacher, notices and acknowledges frustration on the students' faces; she begins to explore the source of this thinking.	Maria understands the importance of attending to the nonverbal cues of student thinking and uses these to begin discussion.	When teachers acknowledge nonverbal cues as indicators of thinking and acknowledge confusion as normal thinking, students make **attempts** free from the fear of being "wrong," a critical factor for **engagement**. Through honoring their **approximations** the teacher has communicated her **expectations** and beliefs that the learners are capable, helping the students assume **responsibility** for their own thinking. These interactions allow teachers to assess authentically and to provide appropriate **responses** and feedback to learners.
Maria: *Jaylen, what's going on over there? You're shaking your head.* Jaylen: *Well—I don't get—the words are weird. Why did he put them* [the poems] *on it?* Ellie: *On the pots?* Multiple voices: *Yeah ... I don't get why ... me, too ...*	Maria notes the nonverbal cue to the student, supporting students to recognize and appreciate nonverbal cues as evidence of thinking.	**Response** to students about her recognition and appreciation of their **approximations** supports them to understand how they are working to make meaning (assume **responsibility**) and how Maria trusts them to work through their confusions (a factor for **engagement**). A belief in learners' thinking and their abilities supports **engagement**. It also strengthens the relationship that is crucial for engagement to occur.
Maria realizes the students are stuck, but rather than adding her thinking to the mix, she honors the approximations of tentative thinking by asking the students to turn and talk with partners.	Maria decides not to include her thinking. She gives students time to grapple with their confusions and to talk with others about their confusions.	Not providing easy answers to students' questions sets up **expectations** of learners that they can be solvers of their own questions and problems. This kind of **response** to a learner increases **engagement** and **responsibility**. **Engagement** increases as readers see themselves as capable.

What decisions might you make next time? How will this affect each of the Conditions?

In read aloud and shared reading, the teacher can continue supporting students to notice their own and others' nonverbal cues of thinking. This supports them to assume responsibility for meaning-making and strengthens discussions.

In these lessons, the teacher can also continue withholding teacher thinking when students are confused and provide time for turn and talks when students are grappling with confusions. This strengthens **engagement** by demonstrating belief in students' abilities.

Teaching Decisions Examined through the Conditions of Learning
#4 (Blank Template A)

Instructional Area:

Teacher:

Lesson	Teaching Decisions	How the Conditions and Processes are Affected by these Teaching Decisions (Specific Conditions and Processes are in bold)

What decisions might you make next time? How will this affect each of the Conditions?

Teaching Decisions Examined through the Conditions of Learning
#5 Some Suggestions for Turning a Theory of Learning into Instruction

Instructional Area: *Writing* Teacher: *Brian Cambourne*		
Condition	**Aspects of the Condition That Apply to Teaching: Writing**	**Some Possible Classroom Strategies** (Note to reader: This is not an exhaustive list.)
Immersion	*Students Need:* • Aural saturation of sounds of written texts, words, syllables, etc. • Visual saturation with conventional spellings, letters, syllables, letter groups, and other parameters of print.	• Tell "stories" of role, history, purposes, rationale, etc., of importance of writing. • Conduct wall print, print walks, shared book (big books) with a writing focus. • Use read aloud and shared reading, in which writing skills, knowledge, and understandings are modeled.
Demonstration	*Students Need:* • Repeated opportunities to witness both overt and covert processes that make effective writing possible.	• Use teacher think-alouds of different aspects of writing process. (e.g., brainstorming a topic, drafting, free writing, leads, tightening, proofreading activities). • Use teacher-led individual conferences and peer-conferencing. • Rewrite informational texts as fairy tales/narratives using the same content. • Model the process of "reading like a writer."
Engagement	*Students Need:* • Constant reminders of the power and value of effective writing. • To understand that writing is not just a tool of communication but also the most powerful tool available to us for thinking and learning.	• Tell stories or share examples that make explicit the reasons for becoming an effective user of writing. • Share one's own (or others') attempts at using writing to clarify and extend our own thinking and learning.
Expectation	*Students Need:* • To believe you are an adult whom they can trust, and who has their best interests at heart. (i.e., you have bonded with them). • To believe that that anyone who has learned to talk can learn to write. • To be convinced that you truly believe they are smart enough to become effective users of writing.	• Share your own writing to present yourself as an adult whom the students can trust—and who has their best interests at heart. • Repeatedly remind students that anyone who has learned to talk can learn to write. • Highlight, share, and celebrate the gems the students produce.

Condition	Aspects of the Condition That Apply to Teaching: Writing	Some Possible Classroom Strategies (Note to reader: This is not an exhaustive list.)
Employment	*Students Need:* • To know and understand that a "successful" text is one that achieves its purpose with its intended audience. • Multiple opportunities to use, apply, and adjust their emerging writing skills and know-how until an appropriate level of competence in creating "successful" texts has been achieved. • To understand and apply the processes for going from blank page to successful text. • To understand and apply the process of conferring or shaping and refining texts.	• Repeatedly draw attention to, explore, and discuss examples of "successful texts." • Negotiate and construct a class contract that makes explicit the minimum number of pieces they *must* "publish" in a given time span (e.g., three pieces per term). • Model the conferring process. • Provide time and space for conferences to occur.
Responsibility	*Students Need:* • To understand that effective learners are independent learners, i.e., they decide what and how they'll learn. • To know how to avoid surrendering control of their learning to someone else (aka the Just-Tell-Me-What-I-Need-to-Learn Syndrome).	• Model the decision-making process to continually make explicit the idea that good learners know how to make learning decisions. • Model and demonstrate examples of "taking responsibility" or "ownership" of learning. • Draw attention to and publicly notice and acknowledge when students take responsibility.
Approximation	*Students Need:* • To understand that "having-a-go" is fundamental to learning. • To understand how "mistakes" help us adjust and refine our knowledge, understandings, and skills so that next time we do better. • To understand that ultimately approximations must become conventional. (See Expectations).	• Explain how baby talk is a necessary stage in learning to talk and how this relates to learning to write and spell. • Cease applying such terms as *mistake, error* and *correct/incorrect* to students' oral or written responses. Instead, replace with the language of approximation. • Honor and respect all approximations. • Never let a chance go by to model and/or share examples of approximations and how they support learning.
Response	*Students Need:* • Positive, supportive responses ("feedback") which support their burgeoning control over using writing to create "successful texts." (See Employment).	• Closely attend to learners' approximations in order to reference them in future demonstrations that contain information or knowledge they've not yet got under control (see "Upping the Ante" in Chapter 6). • Draw explicit attention to salient features of demonstrations that will help learners modify approximations.

Teaching Decisions Examined through the Conditions of Learning
#6 (Blank Template B)

Instructional Area:
Teacher:

Condition	Aspects of the Condition That Apply to Teaching: _____	Some possible classroom teaching behaviors
Immersion		
Demonstration		
Engagement		
Expectations		
Employment		
Responsibility		
Approximation		
Response		

It's often said that a picture is worth a thousand words. We agree. We leave you with our picture in which we've embedded the thousands of words and ideas we've used in our book. We wish you the best as you use this picture to guide the thousands of teaching decisions you'll make for the rest of your professional lives.

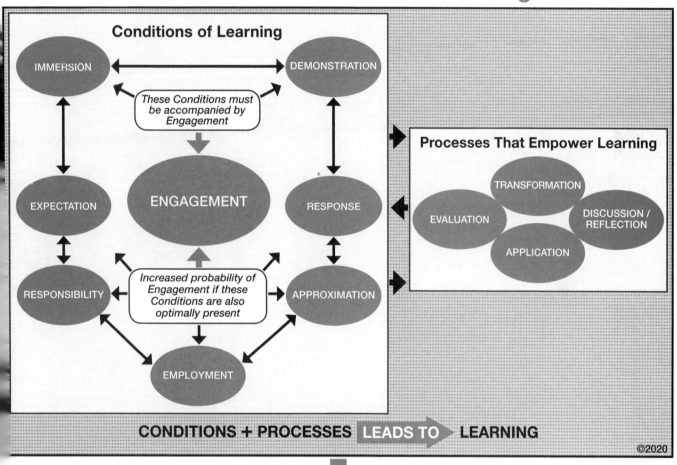

Cambourne's Model of Learning

Conditions of Learning

IMMERSION — DEMONSTRATION

These Conditions must be accompanied by Engagement

EXPECTATION — ENGAGEMENT — RESPONSE

Increased probability of Engagement if these Conditions are also optimally present

RESPONSIBILITY — APPROXIMATION

EMPLOYMENT

Processes That Empower Learning

TRANSFORMATION

EVALUATION

DISCUSSION / REFLECTION

APPLICATION

CONDITIONS + PROCESSES LEADS TO LEARNING

©2020

Learning is our ever-changing knowledge, understandings, feelings, values, and skills regarding what is to be learned.

Acknowledgments

This book has been a thoughtful journey, and there are those whose thinking paths have converged with ours. We would like to acknowledge some of the thinkers who've been on this rewarding journey with us.

Richard Owen was an early promoter of the necessity for this book and continues to be a fierce advocate for sensible teaching and learning. Through numerous Zoom calls and email chains as we collaborated across multiple time zones in different hemispheres, he influenced this book through his questions and observations, his encouragement and reason. We can honestly say we could never have done this without him.

We are so appreciative of our early readers—Andrea Butler, Tina Haselius, Mary C. Howard, Judy Kelly, Suzy Landuyt, Enid Martinez, Nijala Taylor, and Elisa Waingort. Their feedback was invaluable to us as we shaped our writing for readers. Their enthusiasm, questions, and comments led to what you have in your hands now. Every writer should be blessed with such a thoughtful community.

We are grateful to Jose Ramirez for use of the artwork that graces the covers of this book. *Maestra* and *Education* captured our hearts. Jose is not only a gifted artist, muralist, and children's book illustrator, but also a classroom teacher. You can view more of Jose's artwork at ramirezart.com.

Brian:

I was born in 1936, which, in our culture, means I've been retired from fulltime professional employment for quite a while now. One could say I'm at the tail end of my professional career. According to the theory my co-author and I describe in this book, any ideas I've contributed are the end product of more than eight decades of immersion in a range of different learning settings. I was a school pupil for twelve years, a student in a rural residential teacher training college for two, a K–6 classroom teacher for ten, and a teacher educator, classroom researcher, and academic theory builder for about forty. In all of these settings, I've had the privilege of hundreds of thousands of conversations and discussions with thousands of peers, friends, and professional colleagues. These conversations and discussions have continually shaped and reshaped my thinking, knowledge, and values about learning, teaching, and classroom practice.

How does one acknowledge and pay tribute to so many sources of inspiration and support? I can only do it by identifying the different groups and individuals who've influenced me on this journey.

I will begin by acknowledging all that I learned from both the pupils I taught as a classroom teacher and the students I taught as a university professor. What I learned from them laid the foundation for all the research and theory-building I've ever done.

I should also acknowledge the classroom teachers who granted me the privilege of observing and documenting how they taught and what they believed and valued about teaching reading and writing. I owe special thanks to Hazel Brown of Balarang Primary School, and the staff and teachers of Whalan Primary School. All of them taught me so much about the complexities of the transition from academic theory to classroom practice (and vice versa).

Then there are the researchers and theory builders whose work, friendship, and collegiality guided and supported me on my academic journey. Those to whom I owe a great intellectual debt to are Courtney Cazden, Ken and Yetta Goodman, Frank Smith, Don Holdaway, P. David Pearson, Denny Taylor, Allan Luke, Peter Freebody, and Marie Clay (and many of their students).

In 1984, Jan Turbill and Andrea Butler, two classroom teachers turned staff developers (like my coauthor), started me on what was probably the most dynamic and productive period of my professional career. The organizers of a conference we were attending asked me to "fill in" when the academic they had originally invited to do the conference's final plenary didn't turn up. Jan and Andrea heard me fumble my way through a primitive version of the Conditions of Learning. They invited me to join them in applying the Conditions to a professional development program called Frameworks, which, over the next decade, we delivered to many school districts in Australia, in forty-eight states in the USA, in several Canadian provinces, and in Papua New Guinea. Their ability to turn complex theory into classroom practice through the Frameworks program introduced the Conditions of Learning to the world beyond academia. They remain my soul mates, and I'll be forever indebted to them.

Finally, none of what I've achieved would have been possible without the support and love of my wife, Olwyn, during our fifty-nine years of marriage. Not only was she the family breadwinner during my years as a doctoral student, she also raised our four children and organized our family life in ways that freed me to pursue my academic career. Without her love and support, the journey that has produced this book would never have been taken.

Debra:

Rarely in life does one get to express gratitude publicly to those who have shared the journey.

First and most importantly, I must thank all the children who have given me the honor of observing them learn. They help me understand and appreciate what a privilege it is to be a teacher. Their patience and flexibility, joy and wonder fill me with awe. They are our reason why. And, to their teachers, who bravely shared their successes and their struggles, I see you, hear you, and appreciate you. A heartfelt thank you to each and every one for allowing me to learn with you.

One particular teacher I have the great fortune to know, Trish Candia, sets a high bar for what it means to be an educator. Trish, as a second-year teacher, welcomed me into her classroom just so I could study instruction, with no game plan or guidelines as to what this study would look like or entail. Her reflective and generous stance gave me rich opportunities to explore the thinking of an educator who puts children at the center. Her unwavering focus on children becoming strong and kind human beings is a marvel to witness. Trish, I know I wouldn't be the teacher I am today without you.

To my partners-in-all-things-literacy: Maria Nichols is my thinking partner, workshop co-presenter, and buy-the-shoes-cause-life-is-too-short co-conspirator; Cherissa Kreider-Beck has the stamina and braininess every staff developer should possess, and I am fortunate to be in her realm. The two of you are the best, and sharpest, collaborators one could have. Lyn Reggett, there are no words for: Brilliant seems lame, accomplished is an understatement, and inspirational feels like a cliche. Lyn, I value every conversation I've had with you, because I always walk away being more.

Sonya Fleming and Sharon Page are people you just feel fortunate to know. Individually, they are lovely, together a force of nature—thank you, ladies, for letting me be part of your world. Dan Farley, your expertise and encouragement make me want to be better. Nilaja Taylor, your perspective stretches me and echoes in my brain. Thank you for understanding the need for pancakes on difficult days. Jody Neiss, our walk-and talk-excursions calmed and recentered my stressed brain and I'm so grateful for your friendship. Suzi Jakaitis, your grace showed us all how to thrive no matter the struggles. I miss our lunches that turned into happy hours. To my fairy godmother, Pat Eastman, who put me squarely on this path with Brian and, who, along with her husband, Bill, introduced me to the love of my life: Pat, your no-nonsense style in combination with being wickedly smart is unmatched. Thank you for just being you.

To my biological family—my parents, my brother Garry, and my sisters, Diana, Peggy, and Lisa: Thank you for listening to me pontificate about many topics through the years, even ones I knew nothing about and had no business commenting on. To my Aunt Dolly—you are now the sole bearer of the old family stories. Thank you for never failing to ask how the book was coming along.

To my chosen family: Pam Reed, I miss you every single day. Elizabeth Heeren, nothing compares to the friend who accepts you completely yet also tells you the unvarnished truth! Lora Leigh Lape, I don't remember life without you as my friend. Chip Reed, the connections in our lives are timeless. Having y'all as friends is the best gift I ever got.

And, finally, to Terry: You've nourished me, both emotionally and physically, throughout these years, always seeming to know whether I need a hug or a push. Thank you for always having the just-right word when I need it, for forgiving me when my tired brain just stops making sense, and for ignoring me when I become too bossy. You've taught me the meanings of patience and love, especially for a furry little one named Precious.

References

Allington, R. L. (2006). *What Really Matters for Struggling Readers: Designing Research-Based Programs.* Pearson.

Aviles, G. (2018). Lin-Manuel Miranda, *Hamilton* creators awarded first-of-its-kind Kennedy Center honor, NBC News, December 3, 2018. https://www.nbcnews.com/news/latino/lin-manuel-miranda-hamilton-creators-awarded-first-its-kind-kennedy-n943171.

Barnes, D. (2008). Cited in Mercer, M., and S. Hodgkinson (2008). *Exploring Talk in School: Inspired by the Work of Douglas Barnes.* Sage Publications.

Biomimicry Institute (2020). "What Is Biomimicry." https://biomimicry.org/what-is-biomimicry/.

Boushey, G., and J. Moser (2006). *The Daily Five: Fostering Literacy in the Elementary Grades.* Stenhouse.

Brackett, M. (2019). *Permission to Feel: Unlocking the Power of Emotions to Help Our Kids, Ourselves, and Our Society Thrive.* Celadon Books.

Brisson, P. (1998). *The Summer My Father Was Ten,* illustrated by A. Shine. Boyds Mills Press.

Britton, J. (1970). "Their Language and Our Teaching." *English in Education* 4, no. 2: 5-13.

Bruner, J. S. (1973). *Beyond the Information Given: Studies in the Psychology of Knowing.* W.W. Norton.

Burkins, J. M., and M. Croft (2010). *Preventing Misguided Reading: New Strategies for Guided Reading Teachers.* Corwin Press.

Buzsaki, G. (2019). *The Brain from the Inside Out.* Oxford University Press.

Calkins, L. (1994). *The Art of Teaching Writing.* Heinemann.

Cambourne, B. L. (1972). "A Naturalistic Study of the Language Performance of Grade 1 Rural and Urban School Children." PhD thesis, James Cook University.

Cambourne, B. L. (1988). *The Whole Story: Natural Learning and the Acquisition of Literacy in the Classroom.* Scholastic.

Cambourne, B. L. (1995). "Toward an Educationally Relevant Theory of Literacy Learning: Twenty Years of Inquiry." *The Reading Teacher* 49, no. 3: 182-191.

Cambourne, B. L. (2001). "Why Do Some Students Fail to Learn? Ockham's Razor and the Conditions of Learning." *The Reading Teacher* 54, no. 8: 784-786.

Cambourne B. L. (2007). "Biomimicry and Educational Innovation." *BioInspired* 5, no.1: 7-9.

Cambourne, B. L. (2013). "Doin' What Comes Naturally: Using Nature's Best Biological Ideas to Inform Classroom Practice." (Presentation, International Reading Association 58th Annual Convention, San Antonio, TX, April 20, 2010).

Cambourne, B. L. (2015). "Are Teacher Read Alouds the Swiss Army Knife of Effective Reading and Writing Pedagogy?" In *In Defense of Read Aloud: Sustaining Best Practice,* by Steven L. Layne, 17-18. Stenhouse Publishers.

Cambourne, B. L. (2017). "Reclaiming or Reframing? Getting the Right Conceptual Metaphor for Thinking about Early Literacy Learning." In *Reclaiming Early Childhood Literacies: Narratives of Hope, Power, and Vision,* edited by R. Meyer and K. Whitmore, 17-29. Routledge.

Cambourne, B. L., and J. Turbill (1987). *Coping with Chaos.* Primary English Teaching Association.

Cazden, C. B. (1988). *Classroom Discourse: The Language of Teaching and Learning.* Heinemann.

Chambers, A. (1993). *Tell Me: Children, Reading, and Talk.* Stenhouse.

Chomsky, C. (1976). "Creativity and Innovation in Child Language" *Journal of Education* 158, no. 2: 12-24.

Clay, M. M. (1982). *Observing Young Readers: Selected Papers.* Heinemann.

Clay, M. M. (1985). *The Early Detection of Reading Difficulties,* 3rd ed. Heinemann.

Clay, M. M. (1991). *Becoming Literate: The Construction of Inner Control.* Heinemann.

Clay, M. M. (1998). *By Different Paths to Common Outcomes.* Stenhouse.

Cobb, M. (2020). "Why Your Brain Is Not a Computer." *Guardian* (UK edition), February 27, 2020. https://www.theguardian.com/science/2020/feb/27/why-your-brain-is-not-a-computer-neuroscience-neural-networks-consciousness.

Crouch, D. (2018). "Why Revisiting Shared Reading Texts Matters for Emergent and Early Learners." *Reading Recovery,* August 22, 2018. https://readingrecovery.org/revisiting-shared-reading-texts-matters-emergent-early-learners/.

Curtiss, S. (1977). *Genie: A Psycholinguistic Study of a Modern-Day "Wild Child."* Academic Press.

Deacon, T. (1997). *The Symbolic Species: The Co-evolution of Language and the Brain.* W.W. Norton.

Delpit, L. (1995). *Other People's Children: Cultural Conflict in the Classroom.* The New Press.

Denton, P. (2007). *The Power of Our Words: Teacher Language That Helps Children Learn.* Center for Responsive Schools, Inc.

Derewianka, B. (1990). *Exploring How Texts Work.* Primary English Teaching Association.

Dorn, L., and C. Soffos (2005). *Teaching for Deep Comprehension: A Reading Workshop Approach.* Stenhouse.

Dweck, C. S. (2006). *Mindset: The New Psychology of Success.* Random House.

Edelman, G. (1987). *Neural Darwinism: The Theory of Neuronal Group Selection.* Basic Books.

Feely, J. (2009). *Spiders.* From Flying Start to Literacy, Okapi Educational Publishing.

Fisher, B. (1991). *Joyful Learning in Kindergarten.* Heinemann.

Fountas, I., and G. S. Pinnell (1996). *Guided Reading: Good First Teaching for All Children.* Heinemann.

Fountas, I., and G. S. Pinnell (2006). *Teaching for Comprehending and Fluency: Thinking, Talking, and Writing about Reading, K-8.* Heinemann.

Fountas, I., and G. S. Pinnell (2007). *The Continuum of Literacy Learning, Grades K-8.* Heinemann.

Fountas, I., and G. S. Pinnell (2016a). *The Fountas & Pinnell Literacy Continuum: A Tool for Assessment, Planning, and Teaching, PreK-8,* expanded edition. Heinemann.

Fountas, I., and G. S. Pinnell (2016b). *Guided Reading: Responsive Teaching across the Grades,* 2nd ed. Heinemann.

Fountas, I., and G. S. Pinnell (2017). "A Level is a Teacher's Tool, NOT a Child's Label." *Fountas & Pinnell Literacy,* September 29, 2016. https://fpblog.fountasandpinnell.com/a-level-is-a-teacher-s-tool-not-a-child-s-label.

Freebody, P., and A. Luke (1990). "'Literacies' Programs: Debates and Demands in Cultural Context." *Prospect* 5, no. 3: 7-16.

Freeman, D. E., and Y. S. Freeman (2004). *Essential Linguistics: What You Need to Know to Teach Reading, ESL, Spelling, Phonics, and Grammar.* Heinemann.

Frégnac, Y. (2017). "Big Data and the Industrialization of Neuroscience: A Safe Roadmap for Understanding the Brain?" *Science* 358, no. 6362: 470-477.

Gardner, H. (2009). *Five Minds for the Future.* Harvard Business Review Press.

Gibbons, P. (1993). *Learning to Learn in a Second Language.* Heinemann.

Gibbons, P. (2001). *Scaffolding Language, Scaffolding Learning: Teaching English Language Learners in the Mainstream Classroom.* Heinemann.

Goodman, K. S. (1965). "A Linguistic Study of Cues and Miscues in Reading." *Elementary English* 42, no. 6: 639-643.

Halliday, M. A. K. (1973). *Explorations in the Functions of Language.* Edward Arnold.

Halliday, M. A. K. (1975). *Learning How to Mean: Explorations in the Development of Language.* Edward Arnold.

Halliday, M. A. K. (1978). "Meaning and the Construction of Reality in Early Childhood." *In Modes of Perceiving and Processing of Information,* edited by H. L. Pick, Jr. and E. Saltzman, 67-96. Lawrence Erlbaum Associates.

Halliday, M. A. K. (2003). "On Language in Relation to the Evolution of Human Consciousness." In *On Language and Linguistics,* Vol. 3, edited by J. Webster, 390-432. Bloomsbury.

Hawken, P. (2007). *Blessed Unrest: How the Largest Movement in the World Came into Being, and Why No One Saw It Coming.* Penguin Books.

Hebb, D. O. (1949). *The Organization of Behavior: A Neuropsychological Theory.* John Wiley & Sons.

Hill, L. C. (2010). *Dave the Potter: Artist, Poet, Slave,* illustrated by B. Collier. Little, Brown.

Hindley, J. (1996). *In the Company of Children.* Stenhouse.

Hirsh-Pasek, K., R. M. Alper, and R. M. Golinkoff (2018). "Living in Pasteur's Quadrant: How Conversational Duets Spark Language at Home and in the Community." *Discourse Processes* 55, no. 4: 338-345.

Hogenboom, M. (2019). "Why the Way We Talk to Children Really Matters." *BBC Future,* October 1, 2019. https://www.bbc.com/future/article/20191001-the-word-gap-that-affects-how-your-babys-brain-grows.

Holdaway, D. (1979). *The Foundations of Literacy.* Ashton Scholastic.

Hornsby, D. (2000). *A Closer Look at Guided Reading.* Eleanor Curtain Publishing.

Howard, M. (2012). *Good to Great Teaching: Focusing on the Literacy Work That Matters.* Heinemann.

Hoyt, L. (2018). *Crafting Nonfiction Primary: Lessons on Writing Process, Traits, and Craft.* Heinemann.

Ivey, G. (2010). "Texts That Matter." *Educational Leadership* 67, no. 6: 18-23.

Jackendoff, R. (2010). "Your Theory of Language Evolution Depends on Your Theory of Language." In *The Evolution of Human Language: Biolinguistic Perspectives,* edited by R. Larson, V. Déprez, and H. Yamakido, 63-72. Cambridge University Press.

Jobs, S. (1997). "Steve Jobs Insult Response." https://www.youtube.com/watch?v=FF-tKLISfPE&t=228s.

Johnston, P. H. (1997). *Knowing Literacy: Constructive Literacy Assessment.* Stenhouse.

Johnston, P. H. (2004). *Choice Words: How Our Language Affects Children's Learning.* Stenhouse.

Johnston, P. H. (2012). *Opening Minds: Using Language to Change Lives.* Stenhouse.

Jones, S. M., and J. Kahn (2017). *The Evidence Base for How We Learn: Supporting Students' Social, Emotional, and Academic Development.* The Aspen Institute.

Kohn, A. (2018). *Punished by Rewards: The Trouble with Gold Stars, Incentive Plans, A's, Praise, and Other Bribes.* Houghton Mifflin.

Labov, W. (1972). *Language In The Inner City: Studies in the Black English Vernacular.* University of Pennsylvania Press.

Lakoff, G. (2012). "Low Information or High Morality?" *Truthout,* September 5, 2012. http://www.truth-out.org/opinion/item/11348-george-lakoff-low-information-or-high-morality.

Lakoff, G. (2014). *The ALL NEW Don't Think of an Elephant! Know Your Values and Frame the Debate.* Chelsea Green Publishing.

Lionni, L. (1975). *Pezzettino.* Pantheon.

Madson, P. R. (2005). *Improv Wisdom: Don't Prepare, Just Show Up.* Bell Tower.

McTighe, J., and G. Wiggins (2013). *Essential Questions: Opening Doors to Student Understanding.* Association for Supervision and Curriculum Development.

Meek, M. (1988). *How Texts Teach What Readers Learn.* Richard C. Owen Publishers.

Miller, D. (2009). *The Book Whisperer: Awakening the Inner Reader in Every Child.* Jossey-Bass.

Mooney, M. E. (1990). *Reading to, with, and by Children*. Richard C. Owen Publishers.

Mooney, M. E. (2004). *A Book Is a Present: Selecting Text for Intentional Teaching*. Richard C. Owen Publishers.

Nelson, C. A. (2007). "A Neurobiological Perspective on Early Human Deprivation." *Child Development Perspectives* 1, no. 1: 13–18.

New Zealand Ministry of Education (1985). *Reading in Junior Classes*. Learning Media.

New Zealand Ministry of Education (1997). *Reading for Life: The Learner as a Reader*. Learning Media.

Nichols, M. (2006). *Comprehension through Conversation: The Power of Purposeful Talk in the Reading Workshop*. Heinemann.

Nichols, M. (2008). *Talking about Text: Guiding Students to Increase Comprehension through Purposeful Talk*. Shell Education.

Nichols, M. (2009). *Expanding Comprehension with Multigenre Text Sets*. Scholastic.

Nichols, M. (2019a). *Building Bigger Ideas: A Process for Teaching Purposeful Talk*. Heinemann.

Nichols, M. (2019b). "Literacy and Language—Knowing Learners, Knowing Texts, Knowing Practice" (Keynote speaker, Third Annual Balanced Literacy Symposium, San Diego, CA, July 26, 2019).

O'Connor, N., (2017). *A Pizza for Bear*, illustrated by O. Aranda. From the *Lift Off to Literacy* series, Okapi Educational Publishing.

Paley, V. G. (1997). *The Girl with the Brown Crayon: How Children Use Stories to Shape Their Lives*. Harvard University Press.

Parkes, B. (2000). *Read It Again! Revisiting Shared Reading*. Stenhouse.

Pasquale, M. (2015). *Productive Struggle in Mathematics*. Education Development Center.

Pearson, P. D. (2019). "What Research Really Says About Teaching Reading—and Why That Still Matters." *Literacy Now*, October 22, 2019. https://www.literacyworldwide.org/blog/literacy-now/2019/10/22/recapping-what-research-says.

Perkins, D. N. (2009). *Making Learning Whole: How Seven Principles of Teaching Can Transform Education*. Jossey-Bass.

Peterson, R. (1992). *Life in a Crowded Place: Making a Learning Community.* Heinemann.

Piazza, E. A., L. Hasenfratz, U. Hasson, and C. Lew-Williams (2020). "Infant and Adult Brains Are Coupled to the Dynamics of Natural Communication." *Psychological Science* 31, no. 1: 6-17.

Quindlen, A. (1998). *How Reading Changed My Life.* Ballantine Publishing Group.

Ray, K. W. (1999). *Wondrous Words: Writers and Writing in the Elementary Classroom.* National Council of Teachers of English.

Ray, K. W., and L. Laminack (2001). *The Writing Workshop: Working Through the Hard Parts (And They're All Hard Parts).* National Council of Teachers of English.

Romeo, R. R., et al. (2018a). "Language Exposure Relates to Structural Neural Connectivity in Childhood." *Journal of Neuroscience* 38, no. 36: 7870-7877.

Romeo, R. R., et al. (2018b). "Beyond the 30-Million-Word Gap: Children's Conversational Exposure Is Associated with Language-Related Brain Function." *Psychological Science* 29, no. 5: 700-710.

Rosenthal, R., and L. Jacobsen (1968). *Pygmalion in the Classroom: Teacher Expectation and Pupils' Intellectual Development.* Holt, Rinehart and Winston.

Routman, R. (2000). *Kids' Poems: Teaching Kindergartners to Love Writing Poetry.* Scholastic Teaching Resources.

Routman, R. (2018). *Literacy Essentials: Engagement, Excellence, and Equity for All Learners.* Stenhouse.

Sacks, O. (1989). *Seeing Voices: A Journey Into the World of the Deaf.* University of California Press.

Scherer, M. (2012). "Perspectives/The Teacher Proof Myth." *Educational Leadership* 69, no. 5: 7.

Shortsleeve, C. (2018). "5 Science-Approved Ways to Break a Bad Habit." *Time,* August 28, 2018. https://time.com/5373528/break-bad-habit-science.

Sinek, S. (2009). *Start with Why: How Great Leaders Inspire Everyone to Take Action.* Portfolio Penguin.

Smith, F. (1975). *Comprehension and Learning: A Conceptual Framework for Teachers.* Harcourt School.

Smith, F. (1978). *Reading.* Cambridge University Press.

Smith, F. (1983). *Essays into Literacy: Selected Papers and Some Afterthoughts.* Heinemann.

Smith, F. (1987). *Joining the Literacy Club: Further Essays into Education.* Heinemann.

Snow, C. (2009). "Creativity and Innovation in Child Language." *Journal of Education* 189, no. 3: 37-47.

Stead, T. (2001). *Is That a Fact? Teaching Nonfiction Writing, K-3.* Stenhouse.

Tolstoy, L. (2002). *Path of Life,* translated by M. Cote. Nova Science Publishers, Inc.

Tomasello, M. (2003). *Constructing a Language: A Usage-Based Theory of Language Acquisition.* Harvard University Press.

Victoria State Government (2018). "The Four Resources for Model for Reading and Viewing." https://www.education.vic.gov.au/school/teachers/teachingresources/discipline/english/literacy/readingviewing/Pages/fourres.aspx.

Vinton, V. (2011). "What Messages Are We Sending Our Students about Reading?" *To Make a Prairie,* November 8, 2011. https://tomakeaprairie.wordpress.com/2011/11/08/what-messages-are-we-sending-our-students-about-reading/.

Vinton, V. (2017). *Dynamic Teaching for Deeper Reading: Shifting to a Problem-Based Approach.* Heinemann.

Vinton, V. (2020). "Do We Underestimate the Students We Teach?" *To Make a Prairie,* February 23, 2020. https://tomakeaprairie.wordpress.com/2020/02/23/do-we-underestimate-the-students-we-teach/.

Vogt, M. E. (1989). "The Congruence between Preservice Teachers' and Inservice Teachers' Attitudes and Practices toward High and Low Achievers." Doctoral dissertation, University of California, Berkeley.

Vogt, M. E. (2000). "Content Learning for Students Needing Modifications: An Issue of Access." In *Creativity and Innovations in the Content Areas: A Resource for Intermediate, Middle, and High School Teachers,* edited by M. McLaughlin and M. E. Vogt, Christopher-Gordon Publishers.

Vygotsky, L. S. (1962). *Thought and Language,* edited and translated by E. Hanfmann and G. Vakar. MIT Press.

Weaver, C. (1994). *Reading Process and Practice: From Socio-Psycholinguistics to Whole Language,* 2nd ed. Heinemann.

Wegerif, R. (2013). *Dialogic: Education for the Internet Age.* Routledge.

Whorf, B. (1956). *Language, Thought, and Reality: Selected Writings of Benjamin Lee Whorf,* edited by J. B. Carroll, MIT Press.

Wiggins, G. (2014). "A Veteran Teacher Turned Coach Shadows 2 Students for 2 Days - A Sobering Lesson Learned." *Granted, and...*, October 10, 2014. https://grantwiggins.wordpress.com/2014/10/10/a-veteran-teacher-turned-coach-shadows-2-students-for-2-days-a-sobering-lesson-learned/.

Wolfe, P., and R. Brandt (1998). "What Do We Know from Brain Research?" *Educational Leadership* 56, no. 3: 8-13.

Woodson, J. (2001). *The Other Side*, illustrated by E. B. Lewis. Weston Woods Studios.

Index

X–Y–Z

About the Authors

Debra Crouch

Debra Crouch works nationally as an independent literacy consultant, collaborating with districts and schools in designing professional learning opportunities to empower teachers, principals, and coaches as they envision instruction over time, across texts, and among practices. She has been involved in education for the past 32 years as a classroom teacher, coach, consultant, and author. She actively shares her thinking and practices through long-term professional learning opportunities with districts across the country serving children from diverse language and socioeconomic backgrounds. At Debra's website, teachingdecisions.com, educators can view her video and webinar series for Shared and Guided Reading.

Brian Cambourne

Brian Cambourne is presently a Principal Fellow at the University of Wollongong, Australia. He began teaching in 1956 at the age of 19 and spent nine years teaching in a mix of one-room schools and primary classrooms K-6 for the New South Wales Department of Education. In his tenth year of service for this department he entered the groves of Academe as a teacher educator at Wagga Wagga Teachers' College. He completed his Ph.D at James Cook University in Nth Queensland, and was subsequently a Fullbright Scholar and a Post-Doctoral Fellow at Harvard. He has also been a Visiting Fellow at the Universities of Illinois and Arizona. Since completing his doctoral studies (1972), Brian has been researching how learning, especially literacy learning, occurs. He has conducted this research in the naturalistic mode he prefers by sitting in classrooms for many hundreds of hours.